MOONRAKER

Above: Moonraker enjoying heavy seas off Alderney

Moonraker & JCL Marine Ltd

- Colin Chapman's boat industry

Sarah O'Hara

Foreword by Leslie Mogford

Nighthawk Publishing
Halesworth, United Kingdom

First published in 2005 by
Nighthawk Publishing - Halesworth - Suffolk - IP19 0HG

British Library Cataloguing in Publication Data
A catalogue record for this book is available from the British Library

ISBN   1-84280-076-0

Origination and electronic formating in .PDF by
Nighthawk Publishing

Printing by Micropress Printers Ltd.

Contents

Editor's Note

The author conducted extensive research before starting work on writing this important story. During her research, Sarah uncovered many photographs and drawings that had never before been published. Some, sadly, were just not good enough to reproduce even after attempts to enhance them. Other's showed the defects of age and casual storage but were very pertinent to the story.

In preparing a book for printing, tough decisions sometimes have to be made about the illustrations to be included. It has been decided to include some illustration that is not perfect, simply because it shows, even in its current condition, that it is unique and supports the narrative. Where ever possible, the production team have used advanced technology to improve images used in the book, taking care not to modify the story conveyed by the image.

The reader will see some illustration that has been previously only seen by Colin Chapman and his designers. This includes 'blue prints' and a model which had been thought lost but turned up in a drawer as Colin Chapman left them.

Author's Note

I was inspired to research and write this book after reading biographies of Colin Chapman and finding to my amazement that little, if any, mention was made of his contribution to the marine industry. Having spent my childhood at boat shows, and coming from a boating family, I was well aware of Moonraker/JCL and its connection with Colin Chapman. On speaking to ex-employees and those connected with the industry, it seemed that all agreed that a history needed writing. Somehow, I ended up writing it!

My first memory of seeing a Moonraker was at aged 5 years old from Ralph Garrett's Brundall Gardens. My parents moored their traditional wooden sailing yacht there and I happily played amongst the overgrown gardens and in the derelict buildings. I was transfixed by the sight of these beautiful motor yachts passing by on the river (probably on their river trials). I was told by an elderly yachtsman that these were 'gin palaces' and, in my naiveté, I took this phrase as the highest accolade a boat could have and continued to watch for these wonderful boats to pass by.

Some 12 months later, I was bundled into the back of my father's car late at night (my mother was working) and driven to Southampton for him to organise the repair of a show boat for Moonraker – he had started working for the company a few weeks beforehand. This was the start of some of my magical childhood experiences. When my mother was working, I was taken to boat shows, river and sea trials. I sat in the corner of my father's office and trailed after him around the boat yard – both at Bells and the refurbished Brundall Gardens – our family boat being by now moored down river. I could not believe that I was on these magnificent

11

boats that I had admired from the river bank.

I remember being taken on a Moonraker when it was being used as the Press Boat at the Admirals Cup Boat Race. Moored next to us was 'Morning Cloud': the boat of Prime Minister Ted Heath. I had spent some time gazing at this lovely sailing yacht when Ted Heath himself patiently offered to show me over his pride and joy. At the end of my tour, he asked me what I thought of it. I paused before giving it the highest compliment I knew – "Mr Heath," I said in the loud, carrying voice of a 6 year old, "It is a gin palace".

He must have had a sense of humour for I heard him laugh as my crimson faced father dragged me off the boat and bundled me out of sight.

Over the last two years, I have collected and researched information to put together a history. This book is the result.

Sarah O'Hara
Norwich, Norfolk.
December 2004.

Acknowledgements

Firstly, to all the former employees and those in the marine industry who gave so freely of their time, memories and lent me treasured personal photographs. Without them, this account would not be possible.

I am particularly indebted to Warren King and Fred Bushell—the surviving members of the Board of Directors, who, with Martin Church, painstakingly checked my work for accuracy and shared their memories of the era. Sadly Tony Rudd died before he was able to check the technical and engineering details. Colin Gething picked up the mantle and provided invaluable assistance in this area. Also, I am very grateful to the Chapman family who found material from their private collection, including previously unseen drawings of the Mangusta.

Secondly, my grateful thanks to my parents, family, friends and my husband Jon for all their encouragement, patience and support.

I am grateful to my editor and Nighthawk Publishing for guiding me through the final stages to publication of this, my very first book.

I also thank Norwich Cafe Writers, particularly Patricia Mullen and Tom Corbett, who have also given invaluable professional support and advice.

Sarah O'Hara
Norwich, Norfolk.
December 2004.

Foreword

We were, silently ghosting upstream with the new flood tide keeping close to the edge of the channel on Breydon Water in our small, gaff rigged wooden sailing yacht. Ahead, the roar of serious horsepower announced that something fairly substantial was coming towards us - and rather rapidly at that. Probably no more than 45 seconds elapsed before she thundered through the morning mist and into our sight. The Moonraker 350 Softrider swept past, perhaps only fifty feet away. She was making at least twenty knots, the bow riding slightly high; spray curling away from her chines and exploding into a million diamonds splashing into the water a few feet away. The "God" at the helm, taken by surprise, raised his hand to me in greeting. In the nick of time I put the helm up to take the substantial wash on the bow, but before it hit us she was away and gone, leaving only swirling mist and smooth water flecked with white prop wash to mark her passing.

This was 1970 and what I had seen must have been one of the very early production models on engine trials. Little was I to know how this chance encounter was to influence my future sailing plans and in fact the pattern of my future life.

I joined the Company shortly after Colin Chapman acquired JCL Marine. Joining the Marketing team brilliantly led by John Berry, we camped quite comfortably in what is now Bells marina – our office on board two houseboats. The management team led by David Lane, an ex PA Management Consultant had assembled his team almost exclusively from Lotus employees. It was easy to spot the ex Lotus staff, they were the guys who never went home and burnt the midnight oil late into the night.

The mantra was "management by objectives". David, with his seemingly effortless 'people management skills' was the ideal chap to ensure everybody was on side. The drive for quality and efficiency was intense, control of the manufacturing cycle was extremely tight, the hull was weighed two or three times during build. Tolerance on final inspection was a mere 50lb and with a vessel coming out the build process at about 7 tons - this was an outstanding achievement.

In the 1970's boat building in the main was a cottage industry. GRP was by then the predominant building material, but hulls were often grossly overweight and poorly moulded. Internal fit outs were often massively overbuilt and the material generally was not used to its maximum potential. Colin Chapman and his Lotus staff were in the vanguard of glass fibre moulding innovation and lessons painfully learnt from the early Lotus road cars rapidly got introduced at Brundall. The moulding shop was heated and a constant temperature maintained 24 hours a day. Humidity was controlled; all materials and mould tools were kept in the moulding shop to reach the same temperature before use. Glassfibre was cut to templates and carefully laid into the moulds, not an ounce too much. Hulls were placed on moulded trays to cure before fit out. No wonder these boats were light and fast, they were also very strong. This is common practice today, but in 1970 it was akin to rocket science.

The main strength of any organisation is the accumulated skills of its people. The mix of skills at the factory combined with service engineers who could seemingly fabricate anything better than new, perched on a quay side in the South of France, or from of the back of the company van. Couple this with marketing staff who must have been trained from birth selling freezers to Inuits, it made a Company whose corporate spirit was pure magic. Was it any wonder the Company became the largest builders of Motor Yachts in the Country?

Colin Chapman attracted talent like moths to a candle. It must be said he often did not always appreciate the talents his staff had and to run foul of ACBC was an activity not to be encouraged. If favoured you were given great latitude. However, you had better not lose - winning was the name of the game - it was a culture that ran from the top to the bottom of the Company.

The boats that were built in this period, particularly the Moonraker, are still part of my life today. As I look out from the marina office, I can see 5 of them moored in the basin, including a very rare aft cockpit "sportsman". They do not look out of place amongst much younger Fairline, Princess and Birchwoods moored alongside – in fact they still look remarkably youthful! They have carried the years well. Most problems are enthusiast induced and complaints about performance are usually put right by setting everything back to the manufacturers settings. Most spares are available to manufacturers specification, engines of which we rebuild several every year , are a little difficult to get original parts for but we manage and should be okay for another twenty years. Well maintained boats are still much in demand and command a good price. You still find 'wanted' adverts in the boating press for Mamba's and the occasional Marauder and Mystere still changes hands for considerable sums of money. It is a fitting tribute to the designers and builders that so many of the Company's products are still giving countless hours of pleasure and look like continuing for many years yet to come.

How many times after some cataclysmic event in the Company's affairs was it said, "some day a book will be written about this"? I have heard it said countless times and indeed, said it myself on numerous occasions. This book has been awaited for three decades and tells the story that other biographies and books about Colin Chapman have either missed or brushed over. It chronicles the evolution of half a dozen remarkable Motor Yachts, which blazed a trail of innovation. If was possible to manufacture them today, they would still be at the cutting edge with today's technology. The hidden story is the magnificent performance of a unique team of Boat-builders, Glass-fibre technicians, Automotive Engineers, Marketing men and women. Inspired always to seek the novel, and usually better, way by one of the most charismatic and talented men the engineering world has seen.

Leslie Mogford

Brundall, Norfolk. December 2004.

Introduction

Much has been written about the late Colin Chapman's engineering influence on the world of cars and motor racing. He was a colourful and controversial figure who brought an innovative brilliance to all that he did. His death came at a time when he was under enormous pressures, but his position in history has been secured by all of the very positive contributions he made as a gifted engineer. The Lotus Car business that he founded has continued to follow the path of innovation and engineering excellence that he charted.

However, very little – even in his biographies – has been written about his equally important contribution to the marine industry, apart from a mention in an occasional specialised magazine article.

Moonraker is as much a testament to the creative genius of Colin Chapman. Through this Norfolk-based boat build-ing firm, he influenced not only the design and production techniques of boat building nationally and internationally, but also marketing and business structure. This influence certainly brought the UK marine building industry into markets previously dominated by America and influenced the international market through innovative design and strong competition.

The story of this Norfolk-based boat building company not only mirrors that of Colin's Lotus car building firm, but also the history and development of the marine industry in the UK at that time.

As the unfolding story in these pages tells, Colin Chapman was never constrained by established practice. If it worked he kept it and attempted to improve upon it. If it did not work as he expected, he replaced it with a practice that did work.

In boat industry circles

Colin was as controversial as in any other activity in which he engaged. There were many traditional boat builders who saw him as an upstart. There were many who were jealous of the success he brought to an industry long in the shadow of the North American motorboat industry.

Colin Chapman's contributions were not only in engineering. As important as his use of innovative construction techniques, many derived from the aviation industry, may have been, his greatest contribution to the motor boat industry is arguably his new approach to marketing.

Before Colin Chapman, British motorboats had been solid designs, based on proven technologies and built by craftsmen for traditional motorboat sailors. Some yards were notorious for regarding customers as inconvenient necessities that spoiled the result of their labours. A few were even aggressively disparaging of anything that smacked of commercialism. Far too often, British companies failed to sell their products because others were much better at marketing and presentation.

Colin was that rare combination of an engineer and a salesman who was not afraid to promote his products. He and his managers had built a commercial skill, in the sales and marketing of high performance automobiles, that they brought to Moonraker boats. They sold to traditional wealthy sailors, but they also sold to the less wealthy by offering a value-for-money package similar to that employed in the Lotus car business. One of their successes was to bring categories of customer to the joys of motorboating

Colin Chapman was a hands-on manager. He delved into the details of every business he was involved in, but he depended on good managers. Once he was satisfied that he understood the fine detail, his active mind moved on to new challenges. The story of Moonraker therefore follows the story of Lotus, with Colin being closely involved in the finest detail in the early stages, imprinting his vision on the project, and then depending on other to maintain that path.

John Berry   Colin Chapman   David Buxton

Very few photographs of the three key players have survived. No photograph could be found for David Buxton that could be reproduced for this book.

Chapter One

The Beginning

It is rather ironic that the beginning of this significant chapter of boat building history only happened by accident. If a series of co-incidences had not occurred, then Moonraker and JCL Marine Limited would not have built their boats and the UK boat industry might well have had a different outcome than being the thriving international business it is today.

The first was the bringing together of Colin Chapman, David Buxton and John Berry.

In the early 1960's Lotus Cars, established and run by Colin Chapman, were based in Cheshunt London and were having serious troubles with their sales. To solve this, Colin Chapman approached a man called David Buxton, who he had known since the 1950's. With Colin Chapman's blessing he had formed 'Team Elite' which had success at Le Mans in terms of a class win. David Buxton had also been a Lotus Dealer. At this time he had a large garage concern in Derby and, with fellow racing enthusiast John Berry, were competitors with TVR franchises. John Berry was the sales manager at a franchise in Woodbridge and had managed to get the concession for all the American air bases in the UK. Between them, they were responsible for over half of the UK TVR sales.

David Buxton was employed to solve Lotus' sales problems and he asked John Berry to join to help as a salesman. John Berry states that he had to think about this long and hard before agreeing. He was aware of what sort of man David Buxton was and the 'shady' reputation he had. He also had problems with his TVR franchise – in fact both men were having problems and starting to struggle. However, despite his reservations, and largely as the TVR franchise was in difficulties, John Berry joined Lotus and the backlog of Elite cars soon successfully sold.

Secondly was the relocation of the main characters to Norfolk. This happened when the Lotus operation moved to Hethel, Norfolk in November 1966. As car sales increased, the Lotus factory needed to expand and the Cheshunt site was unsuitable. An old airfield at Hethel near Norwich was ideal. Norfolk County Council were very happy to grant planning permissions and other concessions in order to bring business and employment to a rural area. Moving such a large workforce was a considerable task, some employees decided not to relocate, but one deciding factor for those who did was the comparative cheaper housing costs in Norfolk. A big presentation was made in Wolsey Hall, Cheshunt to all the employees to inform them what the move entailed both in business and personal terms. John Berry was one of the last people to move as he liked London, but he settled in Norfolk and continued to do well. After the relocation to Hethel, Lotus continued to expand and became a public company in 1968.

David Buxton had several business interests apart from Lotus and had left before the move. However, he used to come to see John Berry, who lived at Bramerton, at the weekends from his second hand Rolls Royce business in London (he used to keep his cars in the underground car park at the Russell Hotel in Russell Square). The late Barry Sheene, later famous for his motorcycle racing, was at that time David

Buxton's car cleaner and actually asked John Berry for an autograph as he had seen him race cars and was desperate to get into racing!

The third co-incidence was the death of a German Rhine Army Captain, in 1967 just as he was about to take delivery of a boat he had commissioned Vic Bell to fit out. Vic Bell was part of a family firm based at Brundall Norfolk and was a founder Director of Aqua-Bell, an offshoot of the family's wooden boat building and hire fleet concerns, which was using the still relatively new GRP or fibreglass moulding techniques. This commissioned boat was one of Aquafibre's (another moulding company set up by a number of boat production companies) 30 foot mouldings used for the Ocean 30 (AF30) which they had been mainly producing as a hull for hire fleets, with the occasional private commission. Vic was asked to sell it on behalf of the deceased's executors. This Rhine Army Captain had intended to name the boat 'Moonraker', so Vic kept the name and advertised it as such – well before the Bond film of the same name.

David Buxton saw the advert while visiting John Berry and asked him to negotiate on his behalf as he thought it would be fun to mess about on the Norfolk Broads on a boat. The original offer made for 'Moonraker' was rejected, but finally an offer was made that was accepted. The first thing David Buxton wanted to do was to make his boat more luxurious and so he put in soft linings and a stereo, this was very new to boat interiors.

David Buxton only kept the boat for about 6 months. Used to the night-life and action in London, he found Norfolk very boring and the appeal of the tranquil beauty of the Norfolk Broads, even from a luxurious boat, was soon lost. So, he decided to sell his upgraded boat in August 1968 and again asked John Berry to do it for him. He marked the price up and could have sold it many times over. Unsurprisingly, David Buxton could see potential and decided that he liked the boat business. He telephoned Vic Bell to say 'you had better build 6 more as I have taken deposits for 6'. They decided to keep the name 'Moonraker'.

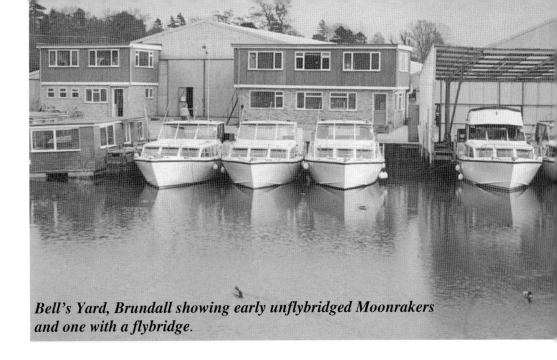

Bell's Yard, Brundall showing early unflybridged Moonrakers and one with a flybridge.

Chapter Two

First Moonraker Production

The original 30 foot 'Moonraker' was born and in production by early 1969. It was commercially produced by Buxton Marine Services Ltd – the production company for 'Moonraker Marine Ltd'. For this 30 foot version, Vic Bell through Aqua-Bell effectively produced the boat for Buxton Marine's orders. Altogether, 52 such Moonrakers were produced using the 30 foot hull – 50 of them in a very short space of time. This confirmed David Buxton's opinion that there was vast growth potential in the manufacture of seaworthy fibreglass motor yachts.

This sudden demand for production, while good for business, caused many practical problems in terms of premises space and staff. Initial planning permission for another boat shed was turned down on the Brundall site. However, David Buxton did not take 'no' for an answer, he appealed against the decision and won, and expanded the production site in

Above: 'Lady Dorothy' originally built for the actor Roger Moore

1970 with a purpose built factory production line at a cost of £80,000! Despite this, room was often a problem on the Brundall site, with additional office space being created by using wooden houseboats that the Bell family had rented out for holiday/fishing lets.

The boat sold so well, that David Buxton wanted to build a bigger one – a 36 footer. To do this, Bell Buxton Boats Ltd was formed, although keeping the original format – so Vic Bell was responsible for production and David Buxton was responsible for promotion, sales and finances. There were 3 main companies within the group: Industrial Marine Plastics Ltd., which manufactured the fibreglass components; Bell Buxton Boats Ltd., which assembled the boats, and; Moonraker Marine Ltd was the marketing organisation. Also involved were: Buxton Marine Services Ltd., which was concerned with the group's internal administration; Buxton Aviation Services Ltd., which operated a company aircraft, and; Progressive Yacht Sales, which sold second-hand craft. Vic Bell states that he was very careful to ensure that Aqua-Bell was kept separate from the 'Buxton' business.

The 36 foot hull was originally designed by Royal Naval architect Robert Tucker who was for a time a Director of 'Moonraker Marine' along with David Buxton and his wife Margaret. David Buxton had decided that he wanted to build something a 'bit special' and Robert Tucker had a definite way of designing a hull – it was always very streamlined and sleek, whilst being elegant and exciting. David Buxton's interior design philosophy was that it should be as comfortable as one's own home. Up until now, this style of interior design and sleek hull had mainly been used in the American markets. However, the 36 hull quickly gained a reputation for coping well with 'head' seas mainly due to the narrow bow which sliced through the waves. The hull design had a sharp 'v' entry which softened to a 15 degree stepped 'v' underside, with a shallow keel aft of the stem. The low rate of roll and pitch this produced resulted in naming this model the 'softrider' which was also the name of the demonstrator. The hull design was patented. It did however give a 'wet ride' through creating spray and water over the decks. In fact, the original hull was slightly modified several times during the building process to reduce the amount of water coming over the sides when facing seas.

The fuel tanks gave it a range of about 500 miles and the boat was a hit with customers due to its interior luxury, its handing and turning ability. One Spanish customer who, having taken delivery sailed straight to Madrid said *"...I am most pleased with the boat which survived really vicious storms.....in the Bay of Biscay, and if only for this (the boat) deserves recognition......One of the storms resulted in heavy damage on the French Coasts caused by winds in excess of 100km/hour as reported by the press....For 10 hours during the night we were weathering the storm on autopilot...one of us keeping watch on deck....and the other two ...sleeping in spite of the bouncing."*

Vic Bell describes David Buxton as a 'workaholic' who would turn up at the boatyard at about 10am and work solid until 9 or 10 at night – often going to 'The Old Beams' restaurant in Brundall for a meal. The two men did get on well, but Vic Bell was aware that his partner had several other business interests and was still heavily involved in the car trade and so was cautious. They had been successful in adapting the glass fibre production techniques to a 'flow line' (reported in the local newspaper in 1971 as "*likely to revolutionise the boat building industry*") and so reduce costs. However, David Buxton was also not a man to listen to advice – this was frustrating for Vic Bell who had been involved in boat building for years. An example of this was the fuel tank - David Buxton insisted that it was incorporated into the hull skin so it was all in fibre glass, timber or foam. A few boats had problems with the fuel filters becoming blocked with fibre glass coming from the wicking of the glass fibre mat or other debris which of course was difficult and costly to repair. In some cases, the only solution was to install a stainless steel tank. There was also a problem if the fuel tank leaked into the hull skin. Some of the early Moonrakers suffered from these leaking problems that only came to light some years later – including the early 36's, such as the Lady Dorothy – bought by Roger Moore and named after his first wife, Dorothy Squires. In the end the fuel tank was made as a separate system, but David Buxton was a hard man to persuade.

David Buxton owned and flew his own plane, he appeared very skilled at this though often scaring his passengers. Once Vic Bell was flying with David Buxton from Holland back to the UK. They had lots of weight on board as they were returning from a boat show, so David had only put just enough fuel on to get back to Norwich. Over the Channel, David Buxton spotted a boat with smoke pouring from it – instead of just radioing the coast guard as Vic, conscious of fuel, pleaded with him to do, Buxton insisted on diverting to fly over the boat several times to see what was going on. As it turned out, it was only a boat burning off chemicals as was then, common practice – but they landed at Norwich with the fuel indicator on empty ! On another occasion, it was heavily snowing and they were flying to Oxford. David Buxton was unfamiliar with the airport and runway they were landing at and it took a little time to locate it. As they began their descent, Vic Bell could see that the runway had only just been snow-ploughed and that at the end of the runway was a huge pile of freshly ploughed snow. Vic still does not know whether, knowing his fear, David Buxton was just playing with him, or it was really a close call, but they ended up landing just inches before the pile of snow.

David Buxton had insisted they had to get to Dover and see a customer, who had a problem with his Moonraker 36, at any cost. They took Peter Willey, a delivery skipper with them and David Buxton flew them down to Herne in his plane before taking a taxi to Dover. Vic Bell was already feeling a bit queasy as he hated flying and the flight down had been very bumpy with the bad weather. Although a good pilot, David Buxton was not so experienced as a boat skipper, but ignored all advice and insisted on taking the boat out to sea despite the near gales blowing. As the boat hit the sea out of Dover harbour, the boat was rolling around in the huge swell of seas. The customer also had his wife on board who was torn between fright and rescuing all the contents of the cupboards and shelves which were falling out with smashing of crockery etc. Luckily Peter Willey had had enough at this point and just pushed David Buxton out of the way, took the helm, controlled the boat and went back into the safety of the harbour.

Bell Buxton Production

One very good reason why the Moonraker 36 was so competitive was that it cost approximately £3,000 less than its nearest competitor, without compromising on the build quality or spec. Speaking in January 1971 John Berry said *"It is because of the advanced production technology the company employ and the fact that we make nearly all our own components that we are able to market yachts at such competitive prices."* Vic Bell, in the same interview states " *We are*

Below: Markida a Moonraker 30 on the River Yare

probably the only company in the country to successfully adopt production flowline principles for a craft of this size." Despite this buoyant press statement, the major advances in production technique really happened under Colin Chapman's direction. At this stage the Moonraker was still being produced using relatively traditional methods – that is one boat was built at a time from start to finish.

At this time, it took approximately 4 weeks to build a Moonraker from start to finish. It started with the making of the hull, superstructure and the great number of fibreglass components by Industrial Marine Plastics which was managed by Derek Shapland.

Once launched (when producing 2 boats per week, one boat was launched on a Thursday and the other on Friday) the boats were filled with fuel and water and their systems were tested. They were given an initial river trial – usually to Bramerton Woods End and back - before the sea trial and delivery to the customer. These river trials did cause some problems as they were often carried out on a (then) unregulated stretch of the River Yare close to the yard. On 14th July 1971, John Berry was successfully fined by the Yarmouth Port and Haven Commissioners for 3 offences under the 1936 by-laws for: *navigating a motor vessel at excessive speed and in a manner likely to cause damage to the river banks, endangering the safety of vessels or moorings and causing annoyance to their occupants.* This incident had happened while testing a Moonraker before it was taken for delivery to Athens the following day. John Berry pleaded guilty by letter and the Norwich Magistrates fined him £5 on each charge and ordered him to pay an additional £5 towards an advocate's fee.

When the Moonraker 36 was ready for production, no more orders were taken for the 30 footer, so all efforts could be concentrated on the new project. David Buxton was very excited about the new 36 foot Moonraker and very impatient. He had booked the 1970 Southampton Boat Show stands even before the boat had been built. It was originally for sale costing £8950 with no tax to pay. Everything was a mad rush, but Bell had a very good team of builders, who worked around the clock to get the Moonraker 36 completed for the show from just the design in 13 weeks (the prototype of the softrider had already been displayed at the 1970 Earls Court boat show at Kew Pier). John Newman was brought in for the sales side, and just as Bell had a good production team, David Buxton had a good sales team although he was desperate to persuade John Berry to join them. It was a job for the production to keep up with the orders at this stage. Again, the volume of production (up to 3 boats per week at peak periods) caused complete mayhem with the logistics of space, staff etc.

John Berry had in fact been plagued by David Buxton to join the Moonraker venture from the start but was undecided. At the time there was a consultant management team (PA Management Consultants of London) undertaking an audit at Lotus to try to improve the middle management performance during a period of rapid expansion. John believed there was a chance of being promoted to Marketing Director of Lotus – so he had initially stayed on at Lotus rather than join Buxton and Bell.

Eventually John Berry realised he was not going to go any further with Lotus. Today, he puts this down to the fact that he was too close to Colin Chapman to have his ideas taken seriously. The Berry and Chapman families used to holiday together 2 or 3 times a year and Berry had believed that they were close friends. However, this 'personal closeness' was a misconception that many managers had. Colin Chapman was very generous and friendly with managers of all his companies – often lending his holiday homes to them and their families and sharing joint holidays. However, this personal closeness only lasted during the working relationship which left some managers feeling hurt and let down by a boss they had considered to be a 'friend'. By now it was 1970 and John Berry felt that he had invested several years and much of himself in the Lotus company and was becoming a bit disenchanted. David Buxton then offered John an unbelievably generous contract: this offered him a salary which was 12 times greater than he earned at Lotus – plus lots of extras such as commission, expenses and a share option. He could not turn this offer down and joined as Group Marketing Director.

Above: Moonraker 30 at Little Venice, London, England

Chapter Three

Moonraker and Marketing Development

One of the reasons why the company, both pre and during Colin Chapman's involvement, was so successful was due to their marketing techniques. They were very keen to create an image that would appeal to their target buyer and were quick to realise that with the economic climate they needed to heavily concentrate on the export market.

Along with the other in-novative marketing men at that time, John Berry had realised that as a whole 'sales' had to change to survive. He developed his knowledge and understanding of marketing concepts with a view to applying it at Lotus. Broadly speaking at that time, most British companies had just changed the sign on the door from 'Sales Manager' to 'Marketing Manager' – there was little understanding of the changes that were happening in business or indeed with the consumers.

In the 60's, most companies had been production orientated – they would make the goods and turn round to their sales force to go out and sell them. This ethos works well as long as the product remains innovative, but as competition becomes stronger – it works less well – as Lotus were finding (although arguably Lotus were innovation and design led rather than production led – a situation that frustrated many of their sales team). The concept of knowing your market and building to sell to it was poorly understood. But in the 60's products did sell, as consumers were probably less sophisticated than today with less product choice available, but towards the end of the 60's and early 70's, things were starting to change.

During these difficult times, Colin Chapman would say "All I want is 1% of the market – can't you get me 1%?". Lotus at this time was beginning to gain a reputation for unreliability. These were indeed tough and frustrating times for the Lotus sales team including John Berry. Lotus was expanding in terms of numbers of people employed and production, but not in sales where the market was becoming increasingly competitive with many other manufacturers building sports cars.

On joining Moonraker under David Buxton and Vic Bell, John Berry's first task was to get himself organised for the August 'Little Venice' Boat Show of 1970. He had gained several years of experience at Lotus doing motor shows – 4 or 5 a year in the UK alone. John Berry soon realised that the way the established boat business sold boats at shows was completely different from how he had managed motor shows and their sales. At a motor show, he would sell an actual car to the customer whereas boat manufacturers would just use the stand as a show piece. John Berry did his research, he went to his competitors, including John Williams at Jack Powles, who he spoke to at Plymouth. He found out that potential customers at a boat show made an appointment to visit the factory to have a sea trial. John Berry was told that you could not actually sell boats at a boat show – you could only generate a bit of interest and publicity. He didn't believe this and decided that he would try and market things differently.

At Earls Court there were two stands available and David Buxton had taken them both to launch the new 36. He got a sales team together that he had worked with before and knew how he worked (Brian Perks, John Newman). John Berry had also researched his target market and agreed with Buxton that they were aiming for the 'ordinary self made business man' type as opposed to often cash strapped boat enthusiasts who only read about them in the specialist magazines. The traditional boat building companies were building for these enthusiasts because they were boating enthusiasts themselves. They were building very practical and functional boats but only 5 or 6 boats a year due to lack of demand. Those who could afford such expensive goods were those who wanted a boat as part of the accessory kit of their success – and no-one was appealing to this market in the UK. Moonraker was the first UK boat to have a radio cassette player and cocktail cabinet as standard on a boat – many in the industry scoffed at this and the other luxury items that are now taken for granted. But it worked, those that had the money, often didn't put many

miles on their engine use – they needed the luxuries on board for entertaining in the harbour. The Moonraker also looked very different with its Tucker designed streamlined hull resembling a giant speedboat. As it handled well, it also had appeal to the serious sailor.

Along with the 2 stands, John Berry had 2 boats moored on the Thames so he could do sea trials there and then and so sell boats at the show ! While his competitors were advertising their boats in the specialised yachting press, John Berry took out full page colour adverts in the motoring magazines. There was only one boat advertised in these motor magazines as the motor dealers flicked through to see what their competitors were up to – and this boat was the Moonraker. These dealers had money to burn and were looking to spend it. Stuart White of Monitor Advertising was used to undertake the photography and brochure layout. Monitor had been involved with Lotus promotions since 1964, when still in Cheshunt. Stuart White had bought a Lotus Elan (number 74) and spent most of his time in Lotus warranty department as it had quite a few problems. As he became known to the staff (including his future wife!) he was asked to take on the photography work.

At the boat show, John Berry took deposits for 22 boats – that was more than any of their competitors sold in a year, let alone from one boat show. His competitors and the boating press couldn't believe it. So as a publicity stunt, John hired the sloop John D – which was moored on the Thames owned by a famous photographer – and held a dinner. He ferried people out to the sloop on the Moonraker, where John Berry had photocopied all the payment slips and order forms received from the show and had them framed and put on the wall. To the industry guests, this signalled not only the arrival, but also the dominance of the Moonraker. Many in the industry didn't understand how they had done it and many hated the flamboyance of this type of boat, much preferring the purist traditional, enthusiasts functional design. Many saw it all as too flashy and trashy – but it worked and it sold. By January 1971 John Berry told the Eastern Daily Press newspaper that *"the number of orders taken since then has exceeded £1.5 million (approx 125 boats)....this*

makes us the largest builders of luxury motor yachts in the country."

Several celebrities bought the prestigious boat, including in April 1971 the French Actress Dany Robin (famous in Hitchcock's 'Topaz'). As she was born in Great Yarmouth's twin town of Rambouillet, she invited Great Yarmouth's mayor, Ken Hammerton, to perform the naming ceremony of 'La Princesse'. In November 1971, Deborah Kerr bought a 'softrider sport' model for their Mediterranean deep sea fishing expeditions.

It was about this time that Monitor Promotions made the promotional video of the Moonraker called "A different way of life" in conjunction with John Berry. Moonraker developed several different models of the Moonraker 36 including the Moonraker VT8, which in January 1971, was the fastest production diesel yacht in the world with a top speed in excess of 35 knots. A number of these were ordered as police boats to patrol the waters of South Vietnam. At this time they were only exporting about 15% of their production but were looking to develop exports by appointing agents. They already had agents in the

Channel Islands, Bristol and France. John Berry also managed to obtain a £98,000 bulk order for seven Moonrakers at the March 1971 Amsterdam Boat Show and was interviewed by the local press as he arrived at Norwich airport "..in the company's Cessna Golden Eagle aircraft, with the orders in his briefcase."

Having an interest in Moonraker as well as his own business sometimes put Vic Bell in some interesting positions. At the first Earls Court Boat Show, they had a Moonraker 36 and Vic Bell also had his own Aqua-Bell 27 fishing/ utility boat there. John Newman was on the Moonraker stand, but as there was a lot of interest in the Aqua-Bell, he offered to give Vic Bell a hand as a potential customer was waiting. John was a superb salesman and had soon convinced the man to buy the Aqua-Bell, but there was one small problem, the man had left his chequebook at home. John was not one to let such a minor matter come between him and closing a sale and he told the customer that this is *'no problem'* we will do a *'house cheque'* – which the customer promptly agreed to.

Later that afternoon, Vic Bell was confronted by a fum- ing woman – who turned out to be the wife of the 'house cheque' customer. John Newman had vanished off the face of the earth, leaving Vic to answer for this interesting sales technique, while the poor husband cowered in the background. Vic Bell just settled the matter by tearing up the 'house cheque' and cancelling the sale.

EXPRESS CRUISER

SPORTS YACHT

EXPRESS SEDAN

Moonraker Class

Cruiser

Sedan

Express Cruiser

Express Sedan

Softrider 36'

Sports Fisherman

Sports Yacht

Chapter Four

Decline of the Buxton Era

The Moonraker was so popular that production could not keep up, and there was a waiting list of 6-8 months. At this time Vic Bell also had a dilemma being a director of Aqua-Bell as it was starting to be a conflict of interest. Although Aqua-Bell had supplied the moulds for the 30 foot Moonraker, it never undertook the moulds for the 36 foot and certainly would not have been able to deal with the demand (hence the creation of Industrial Marine Plastics). Vic Bell was finding the situation at Bell Buxton rather demanding – at this time the production staff alone numbered about 125. As with any business, security is always a problem when dealing with expensive equipment and materials. The Moonraker came equipped with a small black and white television – an expensive item in those days – and so quite a big stock of such Sony televisions were kept in the storeroom. Probably unsurprisingly they went missing so

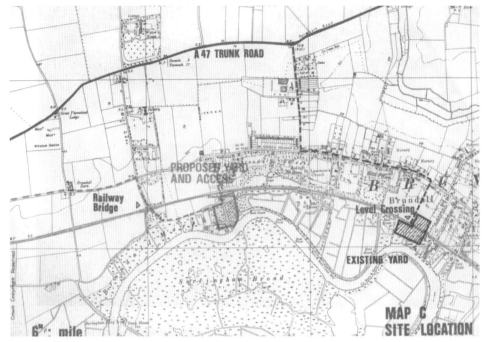

Above: Map showing location of Bells Yard and Brundall Gardens

Vic Bell duly called the local Policeman who, having made his report, looked down from Bell's office onto the factory floor. After spending a few moments watching the workforce he turned to Vic and said '*Well Mr Bell, I can safely say you have more criminals out there on your factory floor than we have in Norwich prison*'.

Vic has since been told that his business kept most of Norfolk supplied with power tools, such as jigsaws! When Colin Chapman's company took over, they transferred a scaled down version of the Lotus security system This was essentially a security 'hut' where visitors signed in and out and this enabled the company to have reduced premiums for insurance, such as fire. The only problem here was that Bell's marina and JCL shared the same entrance and this caused some rankling as security searched everybody !

As the 36 was such a success, again David Buxton wanted a bigger boat, a 46 footer, but this never got into production despite being 'ready to leave the drawing board' in early 1971 at an estimated price of £17 -£18000 per boat. It was about at this time that despite the huge success of the sales of the Moonraker, there were financial difficulties emerging. For whatever reason, even though the Moonraker was selling well and the company

38

Above: Aerial photograph, taken from Colin Chapman's plane, of the site from the River Yare

Photograph courtesy of the Chapman family archive

should have been very profitable, it wasn't. There has been much speculation and rumour regarding David Buxton's involvement in this, although no proof of where the money went, despite (after the sale of the company) being the subject of a police investigation about this and other matters. Vic Bell thought he would be okay as he had very specifically kept to the production and left the sales and larger financial side to David Buxton.

John Berry, as he had feared, started to have problems with David Buxton in the first couple of months, as the cash deposits (many customers preferred to pay in cash) would disappear. There was no money left to pay the suppliers and Moonraker was close to bankruptcy, as companies started to refuse to supply them, almost halting production. John Berry, however, was still in regular contact with Colin Chapman – during one of their ski-ing holidays he got Colin Chapman interested in buying the company.

Colin Chapman's takeover

Colin Chapman became involved with his intention of buying the company - this process was not problem free and was for a while an 'on' then 'off' deal. One major problem was that Vic Bell owned the production site as he had had to buy the premises off his father - apparently his father had not trusted Buxton and insisted that Bell buy the premises off the family to use for the Bell Buxton enterprise. Without the property and boatyard there was no-where to build the boats and so Colin Chapman would not buy the company. Colin Chapman also wanted further land to expand the business. Vic Bell was in quite a quandary at this time. His father, mistrusting David Buxton, had put the hire fleet under Vic's brother's charge, also Aqua-Bell was still producing small utility fishing/day boats with some success. All this, plus the Bell Buxton production was on the relatively small site. The 125 people Bell Buxton production employed were all dependant on the business for their jobs, also there were suppliers needing to be paid. Buxton was one day pressurising Vic Bell to sell the land to Colin Chapman, and the next day changing his mind and, of course, Vic Bell was being put under pressure from Colin Chapman himself who wanted to close the deal. What had grown out of a small family venture had turned into a large business with all the inherent problems and hassles that come with the territory. If Bell Buxton went under, despite trying to keep the businesses separate, Vic Bell realised it would harm his family business. So, it was with great reluctance that Vic Bell sold the business to Colin

Above: Before office renovation at the Brundall Garden site

Both photographs courtesy of the Chapman family archive

Below: After office renovation at the Brundall Garden site

Chapman and leased him the boatsheds and surrounding land. He also sold 3 ½ acres and another 15 acres of marsh-land plus an acre of car parking space to Colin Chapman (in fact to one of the property holding companies).

Vic Bell went to Lotus headquarters at Hethel to sign the land deal and remembers it to this day as it was quite comical. Colin Chapman and Fred Bushell were sitting in their huge office, and didn't seem able to get Vic Bell to sign the contract quick enough. All throughout this brief meeting, Colin Chapman was on the radio phone to David Buxton who was apparently circling overhead in his aeroplane while waiting to land at the Hethel landing strip!

In July 1971 Colin Chapman explained the 're-organisation' to the Eastern Daily Press *"We were approached by the old Moonraker operation to assist the management problems which had been caused by an over-rapid expansion. Mr Lane has been seconded from Group Lotus to deal with these problems, but the financing is a strictly private operation. There are some people who hold shares in the new Moonraker company who also hold Lotus shares, but that is purely co-incidental. Moonraker Marine International has bought the assets of the old companies and will carry on their activities and production. I think the future is very good. The Moonraker craft are a good product and the company has good production techniques which have enabled it to build up in 2 years one of the most important boat building businesses in the country."*

The property company also bought the land at Brundall Gardens Marina (originally owned by Ralph Garrett) which was just up river from Bell's yard. Although run down and needing up-grading, this gave office space and moorings. However, despite the amount of land available on this site, it was not able to take over from the Bell's yard premises in terms of production as intended due to the planning application being turned down in 1971. Planning appeals were also rejected in 1972. The 'Brundall Society' wrote numerous letters to the local newspapers highlighting their objections to increasing commercial activity in the area citing many reasons including: fire hazard, access, additional damage to river banks and flooding to adjacent marshland and hazards from traffic and parking. On the initial application in December 1971, the planning officer described the plans as one of the biggest proposals they had had for some time as it involved some 22 acres of land. The process continued well into December 1972 when there was such public interest that television cameras wanted to film the planning appeal enquiry at County Hall Norwich – this request was declined. The main reason preventing the Brundall Gardens site development was that the access for fire engines was limited by the low railway bridge on the access road.

During the negotiations with Colin Chapman for Moonraker Marine, David Buxton fired John Berry totally out of the blue. John Berry was paid off with £10,000 cash, not an inconsiderable sum in those days, which he invested in 6 houses. John Berry continued to do freelance marketing work for Moonraker - especially boat shows – and continued in his other business interests including establishing Lamborghini franchises. Until 1998, he had no explanation for the sudden sacking and break up of the successful business partnership. Tim Enright 'spilled the truth'

to John Berry. Apparently his sacking was Colin Chapman's part of the deal despite, from John Berry's point of view, their apparent good friendship. Colin Chapman did not want to pay John Berry the £50,000 plus a year salary, when for a fraction of the cost he could move a 'Lotus' man across who would be earning £5000 to £6000 per year tops. Colin Chapman bought the assets of Moonraker Marine and transferred David Lane and Warren King from Lotus to run the operation. Warren King took care of the accounts, administration and paid the creditors from Buxton's account. David Lane was assigned as 'manager'. In fact David Lane had been part of the PA Management Consultant team that had undertaken the audit at Lotus. This company was one of the early promoters of 'management by objectives' which had so impressed Colin Chapman as it was a natural progression from the methods used by himself and Fred Bushell, that he not only introduced the concept throughout his organisations, but also employed David Lane directly. During the transfer of business, David Buxton still came to the Brundall office for a few weeks, arriving about lunch time to have 'brunch' in the riverside cafe, then would sign the cheques for Warren King. In the last few weeks of transfer Warren King went to his home to get the cheques signed.

Fred Bushell then changed the name to Moonraker Marine International Limited – again to keep the continuity. This absorbed Moonraker Marine, Bell Buxton Boats and Industrial Plastics. Vic Bell was kept on for 6 months in a technical consultancy capacity to ensure continuity of production, but declined the offer to remain with the company – and other Lotus engineers were seconded to assist with development. One problem with early glass fibre produced boats, not just Moonraker, was osmosis.

Lotus Cars had great experience and expertise in such moulding and materials and were able to apply solutions to this – so the Moonraker 36 produced after the assistance of Lotus experience soon eliminated this problem. Another problem with the early Moonrakers was that the hull and superstructure were bolted rather than bonded together. As the bolts wore with the marine stresses, the deck would flex

away from the hull. Under Colin Chapman's team, the hull and superstructure were bonded together which resolved this early problem. The 'Lotus' expertise in the area of adhesives and bonding surfaces transferred successfully in the marine environment.

Vic Bell also undertook another project with David Buxton, as Aqua-Bell built a 37 foot hull for him. This had many modifications and David Buxton mostly sold these to the foreign market. Bell ensured that Aquafibre was paid before the hulls were handed over, although, in actual fact, it was often David Buxton's wife Margaret who came to pay Vic the money for the finished boats and moulds.

David Buxton then set up in another boat building business called 'Lancer Marine Ltd' in Oulton Broad in May 1972. For a while he worked with Robin Poulton - who later returned to the Moonraker/JCL fold – producing a boat called the 'Corniche Express'. Initially due to lack of space at Brundall, the Oulton Broad premises had been used for Moonraker production between March 1971 and May 1972, with completed hulls being brought to Brundall by road for fitting out. Again, David Buxton's new enterprise was soon in financial difficulties and he asked Fred Bushell and Warren King to consider buying it and adding it to the Moonraker portfolio. At the time David Buxton had laughed with both men that *"he was good at setting up businesses, but even better at selling them"*! David Buxton eventually moved to Brazil for 'personal reasons' and moved back into the Mediterranean where it is believed he lived until he died.

Moonraker

NOW AVAILABLE FOR EARLY DELIVERY WORLDWIDE, THE OUTSTANDING MOONRAKER
36ft. 24kts. Convertable Accommodation for 6 Adults.
EXPORT AND AGENCY ENQUIRIES invited

MOONRAKER MARKETING, Brundall Gardens, Norwich, NR12 5RG, England
Tel: 0603 713856/714141 Telex: 97286

Above: An advertisement showing the integration of 'Moonraker' and the styalized JCL logo

Chapter Five

How JCL Marine joined with Moonraker — and the truth behind the JCL name enigma

One competitor of the Moonraker was the 'Pegasus'. Although probably not comparable in business terms, it was a boat that potential Moonraker clients would look at before deciding what to buy - it was a product sharing the same market. The Pegasus had raced in the Round Britain Power Boat Race for 2 or 3 years and was a well known sea going boat. The company was owned by a builder called John Colin Leslie Jacobs for whom boat building was a hobby or a side line. His company was called JCL Marine (JCL standing for John Colin Leslie, not named – as some marine journalists have speculated, because 'JCL' was part of the number plate designated to Norfolk!). John Jacobs contacted John Berry, as he wanted to sell JCL Marine and retire. When John Berry went to see exactly what it was that Jacobs wanted to sell, they had one order and the hulls were wooden as opposed to glass fibre moulded. John Berry advised him that in this state, in real terms he was not going to raise much cash. He advised him to market the Pegasus strongly at the next boat show, then sell the company with a full order book. John Jacobs hadn't even booked a stand at the Earls Court boat show at this point. John Berry hired his successful Moonraker sales team at a very high rate of commission and they went off to the boat show. They only had one boat at the show – a Pegasus 35 – and their stand was in the annexe section of Earls Court, rather than a prime site, due to the late booking. In the same annexe there were two Moonrakers in gold fleck – a paint job that didn't set it off to the best advantage – and the boats were priced about the same. The Pegasus was a bit more traditional, having more wood and teak finish in the interior, and was offered in fibre glass or wood. After five days, John Berry had taken orders for eight Pegasus boats.

Colin Chapman had been amazed and somewhat irritated that despite an early booking, they had been unable to obtain a prime position for the Moonraker in the main hall. This demonstrates how the British boat industry at the time worked in very traditional ways. His team were informed that as they were newcomers to the trade they could expect to be allocated a stand within the main hall in about 5 years time. In contrast, JCL, as an established business, would have obtained a decent position if they had booked earlier.

On the last day of the show, Colin Chapman came over to see how things were and John was able to tell him that they had taken orders for twelve boats. Colin Chapman was quite taken aback as his team had sold fewer Moonrakers than expected. Colin Chapman asked John Berry to come back and work for him, but John said 'no' as he had to sell JCL Marine for John Jacobs. Colin Chapman offered the deal that he would buy JCL Marine if John Berry came back to work for Moonraker.

Colin Chapman had one condition – he didn't want to build Pegasus boats – he said that John Berry had to convert the Pegasus orders into Moonrakers. Bearing in mind that most of those having ordered Pegasus boats had been hovering between buying either the Pegasus or the Moonraker, this was not as tough a task as it may sound. John Berry said that he would do his best and went to see those that had ordered. John converted all but one order – the customer that wouldn't convert wanted a wooden boat and luckily the one Pegasus boat (i.e. the boat show model) was wooden – so even that sale was kept. However the way they undertook to convert the sales was interesting .

The Pegasus hull had a steep chine which affected the handling at speed. John Berry or John Newman would take the potential customers out for their 'sea trial' on Breydon Water on the Norfolk Broads, on a particular stretch with a buoy marker used to time speeds. They would open up the throttle and then hand over the controls to the client just before they needed to go around the buoy in the channel. At speed the Pegasus did not respond quickly, so the scared client would hand over the controls to John Berry or John Newman, who knowing how to manage the quirky handling, quickly brought the boat back under control by easing off the throttle. Therefore they fairly easily convinced the client to buy the Moonraker (which handled very smoothly) instead .

Colin Chapman then bought JCL Marine – thus gaining access to a better position in the Earls Court Boat Show with the established JCL name. However, this sale caused a big rift between the two men and arguments dragged as they disagreed about how John Berry would be paid commission for this deal. It is something that John Berry still feels cross about, as when he did the deal for Colin Chapman to buy JCL, the commission value would have bought him 2 Range Rovers. By the time he finally got the money, there was only the value of half a Range Rover. The two men did not speak again until the day before Chapman's death.

From 5th April 1973, JCL Marine Ltd became the trading company for 'Moonraker'. Using the 'JCL Marine' name was also beneficial for two reasons. One was that the reputation that Moonraker had gained for non payment of suppliers under David Buxton's financial management still lingered, despite improved payments under the new regime; secondly as plans for new boats such as the Marauder and Mystere range developed, the 'Moonraker' name was not so relevant. Many of the company cars did in fact carry 'JCL' on their number plate, but this was coincidental.

To run the Moonraker/ JCL organisation over the years, a number of companies were used for the separate activities. Many of these were names that were bought with the companies acquired for their property. From the 2nd January 1974 Moonraker Motor Yachts Ltd was the operating company building the Moonrakers. JCL was effectively the marketing and sales company. Marauder Ltd, formed on the 7th November 1973, built the Marauders. Ludham Plastics (Engineering) Ltd from April 1973, provided the aluminium fittings that were on 90% of the craft produced. Blue Cruisers Ltd was registered in May 1974, and from the Brundall Gardens purchase came 'Brundall Gardens Yacht Station'. Blue Cruisers operated a fleet of six day launches out of these premises for about a year in order to maintain the correct business activity to assist in application for planning consents. Technocraft Ltd based at the Hethel site, was initially called Technocraft Marine Ltd and was the development and research company mainly dealing in the GRP and moulding development. It soon lost the 'Marine' part of the name as it served both the car and marine business.

The JCL Marine Ltd 'Staff Handbook' dated April 1973 states on Page 1 *"JCL was formed in January 1973 to consolidate the activities of Moonraker Marine International Limited and Pegasus Marine. The activities of these organisations are directed to the marketing of sea-going power cruisers, each with its own market image, currently Moonraker and Pegasus......Planning for the future is carried out by a research unit, which combines new product concepts with advanced materials and methods. This unit is directed personally by the Chairman, Mr A C B Chapman, who has received world-wide recognition for his achievements, particularly for winning the World Formula One Championship five times, an unparalleled feat"*.

Above: The Moonraker was to benefit from careful development with new techniques and technologies in production

Chapter Six

Developments

Although predominantly an engineer, Colin Chapman CBE, BSc(Eng), FRSA, took great interest in all marine matters once he became involved in the industry. Hazel Chapman says that Colin had always told her that *"there was no problem that could not be solved, given enough time, research and thought"*. Research and attention to detail certainly appear to dominate accounts of how Chapman approached problems. Although he has been attributed with new developments in the motor and marine world, often it has been through painstaking research, then re-thinking, or re-working an old idea rather than a completely new innovation. Colin Chapman also created a working environment where his employees were encouraged to be innovative – this creative freedom made it a very exciting place to work – a fact which is echoed by most former employees. Time and time again, ex-employees have stated that they *'had the best time of their professional lives'* while working for the firm.

Colin Chapman also took interest in the smallest of design details, such as door handles. Stuart White remembers flying to the Genoa boat show with him, as Stuart was also a pilot he was acting as co-pilot as well as photographer. As he had a Press Pass, he was able to get straight onto any stand and photograph the competitions' boats and Colin Chapman was very taken with the Italian designs (at that time marcasite interiors with lots of detail in design). So, Stuart White would be given a 'hit list' of what to photograph and then, when developed, Colin Chapman would pour over photographs of items such as door handles and adapt them to his own needs. However, he undoubtedly had the ability to approach a problem and find the very heart of it in an incisive manner. Colin Chapman also brought together the right mix of people and good engineers to work on such problems and innovations on his behalf and under his direction.

Hazel Chapman recalls spending many days looking around marinas and boatyards once her husband became interested in buying 'Moonraker' - then spending his evenings reading book after book about boats, often with explosive comment about what he was reading and how he disagreed with it! His family have kept his collection of marine design books which would rival a specialist library in terms of number and breadth of content. Colin Chapman had met boat designer Don Shead at a Formula One race meeting and realised from their conversations that there was a lot of scope for design and engineering development in the marine world which had stimulated his interest. Don Shead was listed as Number 34 in April 2003 in the magazine Motor Boat and Yachting's Top 40 most influential people in motorboating. Colin Chapman does not appear in these listings.

Colin Chapman's business team had taken control by late June, early July of 1971 and he had already started to look at the Moonraker to develop it. He and his seconded Lotus engineers put the slightly altered hull, with altered length and width of chine rails, into production in January 1972 following a number of tank tests. The fuel and water tanks on this version were repositioned and the skeg was re-shaped and extended further aft which resulted in a much improved performance. Measures were also taken to reduce the Moonraker's weight – including the bulkheads being redesigned to be produced along the lines of aircraft bulkheads. That is, with the inner structure having holes to reduce the weight – doors too were produced like this rather than being solid wood. In fact, the Moonraker developed or 'evolved' throughout its production with JCL. The hull and superstructure were bonded together and a great improvement in the effectiveness of adhesives had been made. Bob Cornish, who joined the company as a marine engineer in 1972, describes that the saying *'Glue it instead of screw it'* as indicative of the way anything that could be bonded or stapled rather than screwed was. This was to save weight, as a bulkhead full of screws weighed more than one that had just been bonded. In fact using adhesives had a negative impact on the time it took to produce the boat as using adhesives was quite a complex process at the time. Particularly when the adhesives were used for structural parts of the boat, it was essential that the surface to be

bonded was free of dust, time and heat was also essential for a successful bond – not an easy factor to control in a cold, damp Norfolk boat shed. If the environment was too cold, it took too long for the adhesive to set and if in 20-30 minutes it had not set, then it had to be scraped off and re-bonded.

The method of production was totally changed also – methods used so successfully in the production of the Lotus were applied. The hull was moved between the separate areas – almost as if on a conveyer belt - which allowed more than one boat to be in production at any one time. A fibreglass master mould was made from the original wooden hull and the same principle applied to the other components (for example, fuel tanks, shower trays, bulkheads). A gel was then applied to the master mould, which would eventually be the smooth finished surface. Fibreglass matting was applied on top of this and impregnated with a resin which contained a catalyst that set the matting into a solid construction, with the thickness determined by the number of layers of fibreglass matting used. This procedure was all done by hand so it was quite slow, but the larger components

Above left: Moonraker Mould Tools. Glass Fibre moulding was developing rapidly and Chapman contributed to this development

Above right: Fred Peck and Peter Law used traditional skills in cabinetmaking to produce a quality finish

Centre left: Phillip Thacker works on trim.
Below left: Stanley Baber and George Garrod are seen finishing off.

This combination of craftsmanship and the latest technologies produced boats that were value-for-money.

Centre right: Rob Boulton seen fettling.

Below right: Moonrakers on the production line. Chapman took the same basic approach to boat production that he had employed successfully to build Lotus cars.

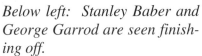

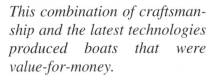

were mounted on specially made steel jigs which were fitted with wheels so that they could be easily moved along the production line.

The hull was inspected before progressing to jig bay one in the production line. Here, the engine beds and engines were installed, propeller shafts mounted and bulkheads fitted. In jig bay two, all the joinery and furniture were fitted with the electrical wiring and fittings. The superstructure was going through the same process in its jig bays, with the windows and trim before the two parts were bonded together before moving on to the final finishing bay. With Moonraker, most of the process was undertaken in the factory, whereas other boat builders finished the boat when it was in the water and this took twice as long. Many traditional boat builders were horrified that a car manufacturer had come into their industry and was applying the same production line techniques. Colin Chapman and his team did meet with an amount of hostility and non cooperation from this quarter. Despite this, these methods made the production cheaper and the process more controlled and so very successful.

As a marine engineer, Bob Cornish regards Colin Chapman's application of engineering principles to the marine industry as innovative. Many from inside the industry hated the fact that a car manufacturer was challenging long held ideas. The way the Moonraker hull was handled during moulding was very revolutionary – even by today's standards. The mechanism holding the hull moulds allowed the hull to turn, so the person did not have to get into the hull to work, but could work from outside the moulds. First the moulds were worked on one side, then, once dry, the hull moulds were tilted the other way for the other side to be completed.

Before Colin Chapman had commissioned Don Shead to design the Marauder, he had tried to re-design the Moonraker propshaft to make it lighter and gain an extra 2 knots of speed. The new design had some implications on handling, but Colin Chapman became totally committed to resolving these in order to make it lighter. He spent some considerable money in order to redesign the propshaft, making it lighter, but the resulting prototype designs by his engineers actually made the Moonraker two knots slower ! Other improvements however were very successful.

There were many variations of the Moonraker 36 available, in 1972 most types carried the '350' badge to denote the combined engine power. However, for a short lived time, fly-bridged models were denoted 900 and non-flybridged 700. In 1972 there were 3 main types of Moonraker 36 on offer:

- Sedan – (aft cabin, open wheel house)
- Cruiser – (aft cockpit, open wheel house)
- Sports Yacht – (enclosed wheel house/deck saloon, fly bridge, aft cabin).

The Sedan and the Cruiser were powered by twin Perkins 6.354 115bp, 6 cylinder diesel engines, whereas the Sports Yacht by turbo charged T6.354's with 175bp. The more powerful engines were available in the Sedan and the Cruiser in a higher spec version called the 'Express' and most buyers did in fact opt for this extra engine power. Customers could have engines of their choice put in their boat and there were also Moonrakers produced with Ford based (Sabre) marine engines – these were different from the contra rotating Perkins in that they were uni-rotating and so required a different gear box with an extra cog to reverse the propeller. The Ford-based engine was slightly lighter than the Perkins. Some early models were produced using either the Bedford-based or Mercedes-based engine, but the vast majority had the Perkins engine.

Some early aft cabin craft were called GT or GTS, which denoted whether they came with, or without, the second toilet/shower compartment. There were successive models labelled as series C, D, E and F as throughout its production the Moonraker developed. After the modifications to the spray-rails and chine, this mainly involved changes to the interior layout. Different colour hulls were added to the possible options from 1972 – the first being yellow.

'Jenjo' was the first 700 model to have a solid cockpit top as opposed to the canvas one. In fact, 'Jenjo' was a customer's boat that returned to Brundall to have the solid top fitted. One of the most obvious visible changes under Colin Chapman's ownership was the addition of the flybridge and changes to the rear cabin design.

The 'D' series was introduced at the September 1973 Southampton Boat Show which had extended the forward cabin windows thus giving greater standing room. The chine had been adapted to give this model a much drier ride than its predecessors.

What was very unique was that the Moonraker, and indeed all of the models produced by Moonraker/JCL, came equipped with everything the customer would need. They worked on the assumption that the customer could just arrive to collect their boat and cruise off. Customers were told that all they needed was their charts, clothes and food. Therefore the boats came equipped with spares, a first aid kit, a torch, mop, boat hook and even an Almanac. As many customers were first time boat owners, this was probably a correct assumption, as they would not realise they needed the equipment until the occasion arose. However, what most impressed the customers was the provision of a cassette player and television as standard !

The exact numbers of Moonraker 36's which were produced by JCL between 1971 and 1980 when they went into voluntary liquidation are not available as records were destroyed when the Brundall Gardens' offices burnt down after being struck by lightning on 15th August 1993. From records that still exist, by April 1979 384 Moonrakers had been built and sold. There has been some confusion regarding the numbering of the Moonraker, especially as according to the press, the first Moonraker (build number) registered with the Lloyds' Register Building Certificate was '467'. Hull numbers for Lloyds were moulded into the transom, but there were also 'build numbers' which were not necessarily the same. Anecdotal evidence suggests that the first 'Moonraker' was actually hull numbered 100 or 101 as it made the boat look more successful than if the hull numbering started at '1, 2' etc. However, it may also be that these were the allocated numbers given by Lloyds Register. The Moonraker continued to develop with several different models, such as the Moonraker G.T. 350 'C' which created much interest at the September 1972 Southampton boat show. This model had a basic price of £15,000 and helped towards the 14 boats ordered worth some £250,000. The 'GTS', when covered by the LRBC contributed to a European order worth £1.5 million pounds, announced by John Berry in October 1974. Fifteen of the GTS's were ordered from Germany and the effect of inflation is demonstrated as the basic cost was now £30,000. A steep rise, even allowing for the increased cost of an upgraded model. The British market was attractive to the Europeans, partly due to the pound becoming cheaper.

One of the main areas that Colin Chapman wanted to develop was the moulding of the hull to which it was intended to transfer knowledge gained from car production to the marine environment. Up until this point, the production was slowed by the need to hand finish the hulls – and there was always the weight issue – this was one area that obsessed Colin Chapman throughout his dealings with both boats and cars due to the impact on speed. The basic lay-up of glass fibre on a Moonraker was 25oz on the bottom and 11oz from the chine upwards. In fact all hulls were weighed after completion and with the Moonrakers, they came within 50lb of each other – which for a boat weighing several tons is remarkable.

A new system allowed for swifter and lighter production.

This was termed a 'spray lay up process' as the fibreglass was sprayed. First the pigmented gel coat was applied followed by a single layer of pigmented mat. Then the sprayer deposited glass to the required weight up to the first layer of rovings. A further layer of resin and glass bonded this layer to the next woven roving and then the final layer of glass was applied. The glass fibre was now carried by a gun which deposited glass and resin simultaneously. This spray lay up was a fast process, but did require an expert operator to do it. Quality Control therefore became an integral part of production and indeed Moonraker was the first boat to acquire the Lloyds certificate. The moulds were replaced after producing about 100 boats.

Colin Chapman and his team at Technocraft (based at the Hethel site) developed the moulding technique still further in 1973 and licensed their patented VARI (vacuum assisted resin injection) system of moulding for marine use. This method had been developed for Lotus production with great success. The idea of using this system was mainly to reduce the weight of the boat (Colin Chapman realised that most of a boat's weight was in the hull)

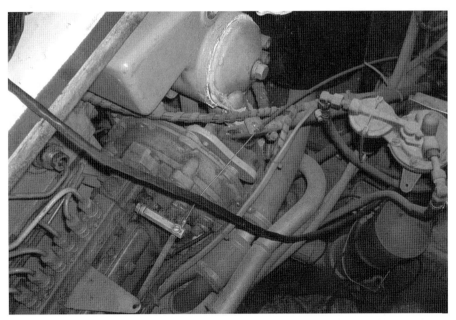

Above: Marauder engine showing how it was suspended on space frames.

Photograph courtesy of Andy Hayward

and to speed production. This system had two moulds, an outer and an inner with the resin being injected under vacuum into the space between the mould skins. The inner mould had locating bobbins (die cast) on which to accurately place the bulkheads, engines etc. When the two moulds were put together, all the air was sucked out and at a given moment, the fibreglass rovings were injected with the resin - the vacuum drawing it from the bottom to the top of the mould. Martin Murray, project manager when interviewed in May 1973, discussed how they had experimented for nine months at

Hethel to develop moulding techniques which traditionally had been heavily dependent on the human element and therefore the standard of the product was variable. Technocraft built the initial moulds and tools for such production.

As with any new technology, there were a few problems initially. Colin Gething who headed the design team (Technocraft) explained how the technique was initially tested using coracles in 4 foot tanks to recreate conditions. The design team consisted of Colin Gething, who had no previous marine experience; Ian Jones who was the Chief de-

59

signer and transferred from Lotus Cars, John Standen was in charge of procurement and Malcolm Leeds who had been with Moonraker and also had experience with concrete hulls. Much unseen research and development went into this and other design innovations, including the bulkheads. As the design team were separate and remote from the production process (apart from the relatively short period when both were based at Hethel), the production team often did not see or understand the process or thinking behind it. It is therefore not surprising that there were some criticisms and differences of opinion between the two different disciplines.

One initial problem with adapting the VARI process to marine use came with hull shape. Under vacuum, when the air is sucked out the resin flowed in to follow the air extract. This is fine with a wine glass shaped hull (like many traditional yachts) where there are no corners, so the resin would fill smoothly and have few or no problems. However, with a chine boat (built with ridges etc) the resin did not run smoothly. This resulted in an attempt to try and solve the problems Bleed points were put in the moulds – the problems with the hulls tended to be at these points. Although VARI principles had been used very successfully in the production of Lotus Cars, some are of the opinion that it was the actual size of the boats and amount of resin used that caused problems due to the heat produced in the catalyst stage. The development of this all cost an enormous amount of money as did the increased cost of production, which was made more complex by this method. Many traditional boat builders felt that this was a waste of time and another example of the folly of a 'car man' interfering with boat production. Indeed, there was a lot of criticism of the technical advances and any failings, even in the prototypes, was taken by the critics as proof that they were right.

The sales team took orders in the region of 10 to 15 Marauders when it was launched at the boat show, where the display boat was a mock up and looked stunning. However, it took about 18 months to deliver it to customers - a delay that the members of the board of directors say was 'for commercial reasons'.

When the Marauder finally went into production, after the hull was moulded the first things installed were the engines (on the space frames), stern gear etc. Next came the structural bulkheads before the superstructure was put into place on the locating rivets. The berths and cabins were then fitted out.

The Moonraker however, was never produced using the patented VARI system. Lloyd's Register of Shipping announced its L.R.B.C. (Lloyds's Register Building Certificate) specifically to cover the design and production of private yachts and small craft on 16th September 1974, to coincide with the opening of the Southampton Boat Show. Lloyds had been working for some years to provide a stringent new set of regulations to improve the standards of manufacture of the smaller vessels. The Moonraker 36 was the first boat to comply and receive such certification. At the announcement Maurice Jobling, (Principal Surveyor for Yacht and Small Craft, Lloyd's Shipping Register) was quoted as saying *"Working with professionals, my staff have arrived at specific requirements which should set the standard for industry. We have been closely associating for the last 9 months with Moonraker engineering, design, production and quality control staff to finalise the standards required for this new certificate."*

On the 20th August 1975, JCL/Moonraker Marine International Ltd became the first boatyard in the country to hold the Lloyds Register of Shipping quality control certificate. Robert Huskisson, Lloyd's Chairman, presented the certificate to Fred Bushell at Brundall saying *"the underlying principle which Moonraker has as its motto is that quality must take precedence over everything and certainly quality every time takes precedence over quantity. I feel there is perhaps a lesson here for manufacturing industry throughout the country and Moonraker is much to be congratulated on having set this outstanding example."*

Despite the initial problems with the VARI technique, Lloyds approval was also obtained for this form of production and every boat that was sold had a Lloyds certificate.

1974 Earls Court Boat Show

This boat show is firmly imprinted on several people's memories as it was the one

61

where an IRA bomb exploded
on the Saturday. A Moonraker
was showered and embedded
with broken glass, wood, it's
aerial sliced in half and radar
cover shattered by the explo-
sion on the adjacent stand of
James and Caddy Ltd. Al-
though John Berry described
the damage as *'nothing serious'*, it cost JCL Marine
£60,000 in lost sales. Apparently, one customer was having
his contract typed, ready to
sign, when the bomb warning
necessitated immediate evacua-
tion of the area – he never returned to complete the sale.
Like wise, 2 other customers
who were due to return to the
stand to sign their contracts did
not return. It says much for the
organisation of the company
that immediately the hall was
evacuated, the staff at the factory were preparing spare parts
for the boat and were ready to
drive them to London as soon
as the extent of the damage was
known. By 10am the following
morning, when the hall re-
opened, the Moonraker was repaired and in almost show condition.

Above: Colin Gething in the design office at Ketteringham Hall, a beautiful Elizabethan Manor House.

©Ron Middleton, Focalpoint

Chapter Seven

Management Style

Colin Chapman put many of his Lotus people into Moonraker. His method of working was by 'accounts', which fitted in well with the 'management by objectives' methods introduced by David Lane.

The system of 'management by objectives' applied to the whole business, giving a profit plan and greater insight and ownership of how the business worked for each manager. For those waged employees, part of their remuneration was dependant on bonuses earned through the Profit Sharing Scheme. However for many of the sales staff, who did not earn a salary but were purely on commission and bonuses, this was fine during a good sales period, but when sales declined or were delayed as with the

Marauder, it had obvious financial hardships. The whole payment structure was quite innovative in terms of incentive and bonus schemes. Chapter 8 of the April 1973 JCL Staff Handbook devotes itself to explaining the Profit Sharing Scheme, stating that it was *"...geared to Profitability and Quality.."* It also states *"The objective is not to work harder but smarter."*

Each department was given its own budget and was accountable for it, so managers of their own departments were really in control – and accountable – and day to day decisions were down to the individual managers. Colin Chapman had to approve the plans such as the annual projections and budgets. Initially here was a monthly meeting attended by Colin Chapman, where the manager of each department had to stand up and give an analysis of their department's performance. Although the monthly meetings continued, Colin Chapman did not always attend due to his business commitments elsewhere. This concept, although now commonplace business practice was a very new management concept and made for a very lean, efficient organisation.

The Chairman's message in the front of the Staff Handbook read.... *"We recognise that a business must provide a vocation and prosperity for its workpeople, together with an economic return for its shareholders.*

We feel that this can best be achieved by ensuring that our enterprise is conducted with the maximum efficiency and profitability, so we can finance the continuous expansion of our markets, our facilities and our employees' prosperity.

This is our pledge to our employees that we will always strive to be in the van of progress in all matters relating to the TERMS, CONDITIONS, AMENITIES and OPPORTUNITIES for all employees.

Such a programme, however, is possible only with mutual trust and co-operation needed in any joint venture...." One of the main marketing strategies was the creation of the image, again a common concept in modern product placement, but very new during this time. The salesmen had to 'sell the dream', and at all costs give the customer the impression of perfection. To quote the Staff Handbook *"Our reputation has been established by the design and manufacture of quality high performance vessels. This reputation can be maintained and enhanced only by the personal recommendation of satisfied customers. We rely on you, as part of a team, to carry on this reputation, to be proud of your work, and help to increase sales, both at home and abroad. We operate in a very prestigious market in which the customer, on a world-wide basis, has a wide choice of outlets for the type of product we offer. ..... we can offer unsurpassed technical expertise, quality of the product and service.."* Even such details as where in a magazine their advert was placed was a crucial issue. John Berry would insist on it either being on the back page (he said that as the magazine was tossed to the side, it had a 50% chance of landing with their advert facing up) or just inside the front cover.

Colin Chapman had also decided that each model of boat should have its own separate sales team, identity and telephone number. He apparently became quite obsessed with this at one point, to the extent that if a customer phoned for a Moonraker and then wanted to enquire about a Marauder or Mystere, they would be asked to phone the separate number for that particular boat. This did seem slightly odd as the cus-tomer would often phone this other number and then start talking to the same sales person who had been discussing the Moonraker with them. Colin Chapman also refused to put measurements of the interior layout in the boats brochure, which did make it difficult for both salespeople and clients who often wanted to know how big a certain cabin was. However, this did mean that the sales brochure did not have to be changed when small changes were made in layout.

Peter Atkins states that he personally dealt with Colin Chapman, taking him out on the boats when he initially took over the company and it was through this contact that he moved into quality control which became a key department. Quality Control ruled everything and could over-rule anybody but Colin Chapman himself. The QC dept signed off all the work in stages and signed the quality control tickets. The quality control department was also tasked to improve the boat and fault solve without increasing the production costs. They dealt with all the customers' faults and were responsible for finding solutions. At that time, Ted Brewster was in charge of the engineering side. David Lane, the

Managing Director, then put Peter Atkins in charge of warranty with a monthly budget and he had to see the people who had faults and put them right. Peter Atkins describes this as the best time of his life in terms of work *"....... I enjoyed it because I was using my brain and was challenged. I think that we did get the boat much better and made great improvements."*

When Leslie Mogford joined the company in early 1971, originally as 'Marketing Assistant' with John Berry as his line manager, he states that he was excited by this very vibrant, forward thinking organisation. He was excited that this company was actually using concepts such as 'marketing' and 'management by objectives' that he had just been taught about and practising them at the sharp edge of the export markets. He had just completed his Management diploma where his tutor had worked with David Lane in London.

Put simplistically, the company's objective was to make money by selling boats. The marketing department would sit down at the beginning of the year and decide the best medium to promote their product – which boat shows and which advertising. They would then decide how much money they needed to support this – including having to order and pay the production department for boats to display at boat shows. By using these methods everything was measurable and controllable.

One of the main emphases was on the export market as the economic climate in Britain was not conducive to domestic sales. Agents were appointed for foreign markets – such as Rene Van Dorst who was the agent in Belgium and the Netherlands. He was also a Chrysler dealer and for a time was involved in Formula One motor racing. Much marketing effort was put into expanding the export market – at every boat show 'good looking' sales women were employed who were fluent in several languages to maximise sales opportunities. With this emphasis on exports – especially Europe, arrangements for servicing the boats had to be made. Mobile service teams were established who operated in Europe, from specially equipped vehicles from April to October each year.

Above: A typical publicity photograph of a Moonraker, appealing to romance and adventure.

Plate I

**Marauder brochure showing a Marauder at speed
and two Marauder interiors**

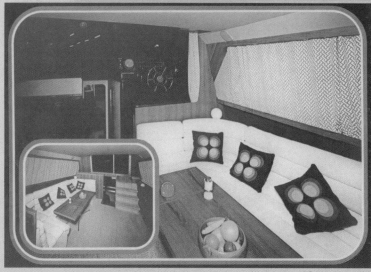

Plate II

Above: Softrider with Royal Navy recruitment display trailer in the background, 1971.

Below: Moonraker 72 brochure cover showing the yellow hull and detailing.

Plate III

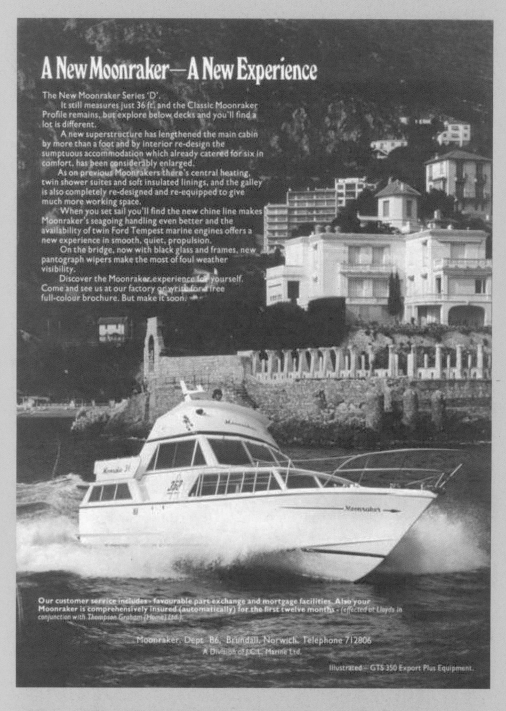

Above: The Moonraker New Experience advertisement set the standard for promotional material. The format is still in common use for luxury express cruisers more than thirty years later.

Plate IV

Above: A colour sketch of the Mystere for brochure artwork.

Below: A Mystere on a speed run across Breydon Water, one of the few stretches of water in the Broads network with no speed restrictions and periods with little traffic.

Plate V

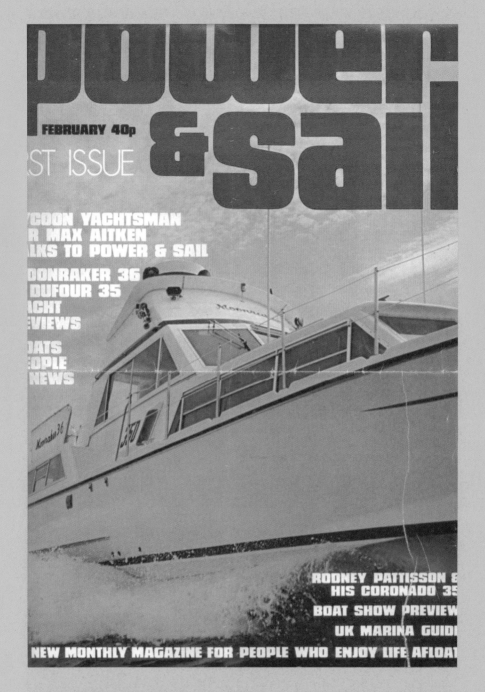

Above: Moonrakers became popular cover shots for motorboat and yachting magazines. This issue of Power & Sail was typical and due in no small part by carefully targeted marketing and availability of professional action photographs.

Plate VI

Above: Mirage interior.

Below: Mystere interior.

Above: Super 36 interior.

Below: Mystere interior.

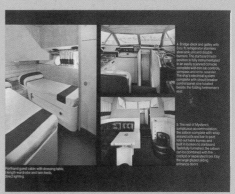

Looking at photographs of the interiors of Moonraker models and the Mamba (seen right on Breydon Water) it can be difficult to appreciate how far ahead Moonraker was more than thirty years ago. The designs would stand up well today, but when they first appeared they were light years ahead of the competition.

Above Left: Moonraker interior.
Above Right: Marauder interior.

Plate VII

Tranquility and action.

Above: A marauder at night

Left: a Moonraker head on

Plate VIII

RAF trained, Colin Chapman was an accomplished pilot and used company planes extensively. Hazel Chapman was responsible for persuading him to switch from single to twin engine aircraft.

Chapter Eight

Colin Chapman and Flying

Due to his various interests, from Formula One racing to his road car and marine interests – Colin Chapman had to be able to travel from different countries at the drop of a hat and it was easier in terms of time and money to fly himself. There are many stories that his various passengers tell of Colin's prowess at the controls. As he had been trained to fly with the RAF (ATC), there is no doubt that Colin Chapman was a very skilled pilot. However, like his predecessor David Buxton, he used his skills to their fullest extent, sometimes causing his passengers an anxious time.

Hazel Chapman states that when she first got in a car with her husband, she thought they would die in a car. Then when she got in a plane with him she thought they would die in a plane – but when she got in a boat with him at the helm she KNEW they would die on a boat! Having witnessed her husband at the helm, Hazel insisted that they had a qualified skipper with them when they went out to sea. She was also the person indirectly responsible for Colin going from a single to twin engined plane. She did not like the fact that they were reliant on one engine when they flew over quite a large expanse of sea to their holiday home in Ibiza and so refused to go again until they upgraded the plane.

Peter Atkins flew with Chapman to go to Portsmouth. Colin Chapman had just told him to be at Hethel (they used to fly from Hethel) at a certain time. Colin Chapman came quite literally with all 4 tyres screaming in his Range Rover, and Hazel and his son Clive were also there. Colin Chapman screeched to a halt just in front of the hanger. "Get in" was all he said to everyone. Hazel went into the back, Clive sat next to his father. Peter Atkins swears this happened exactly as follows ..... Colin Chapman started the engine and moved off immediately, spun the plane around, went to the end of the run way and took off. From arriving by car to take off was well under 5 minutes, no pre flight testing or anything. They had been in the air for several minutes, when the gate house at Hethel (who were the ones who informed Norwich airport of Colin Chapman's flight movements) came on the radio and said *"Good morning Mr Chapman, I've spoken to Norwich airport, you are now cleared to taxi to the runway and then to progress to take off"*.

On another occasion, Peter Atkins was flying with Colin Chapman over the Alps from Genoa, again in a small twin engined plane, there was also a pilot with them but Colin Chapman was at the controls. Genoa's landing strip meant that you had to fly out over the sea to be able to gain enough height to get over the Alps. Colin Chapman took off and rather than circle around over the sea, headed straight towards the Alps. Peter Atkins heard the pilot through the headphones say *'Mr Chapman, you need to circle to get more, height, MR CHAPMAN, I DO NOT THINK WE ARE GOING TO MAKE IT'*. Colin Chapman made no reply and continued his route. Peter Atkins felt that the wheels of the plane could touch the snow on the ground below them and could see the rocks raising steeply ahead of them. Colin Chapman then swore, said 'we are not going to make it' and steeply swerved the plane around to take the conventional flight path.

Colin Gething remembers the sheer energy Colin Chapman had and how he was always on the move, physically and creatively. At the airport from the Genoa boat show, he had given Colin Gething a handful of all the passports for those travelling on his plane, with the instructions to get them cleared by customs. This Colin duly did, only to see that in the meantime his boss had started to taxi his plane down the runway, leaving Colin Gething to literally run and jump aboard the plane before it took off. This was in the days before Colin Chapman had his pressurised aircraft and it necessitated using oxygen masks at height. This return flight necessitated flying over the Alps - one of the team was blissfully asleep and had turned quite navy before his colleagues woke him up by strapping on his oxygen mask.

Colin Chapman had converted his 6 seated Navajo plane to take 7 by removing the toilet. On a 3 ½ hour flight, this meant that everyone arrived rather cross legged ! On this particular occasion they arrived at Genoa for the boat show to find that there were no hire cars available apart from one very small Fiat 127. Somehow 7 men crammed into this car (3 in the front and 4 in the back) and Colin Chapman drove with it one hand, with somebody else changing gear, to the boat show. On arriving, there was no parking and the Italian police were waving people on. Colin Chapman just drove straight up to the front entrance, parked the car on the pavement and, after helping prise everyone out of the car (to the amazement of the onlookers) just left it there. *"We'll take a taxi back"* was all he said. After the Genoa boat show, Stuart White was in Colin Chapman's plane as they flew back to Hethel. Although everyone was tired and wanted to go home, Colin Chapman was still buzzing with adrenaline and insisted that they all go to his house for a de-brief. They sat in his kitchen while Hazel made them coffee and listened to what he had to say, then suddenly he went out, the others were not sure whether he had gone to get something or the meeting had ended. He then reappeared in his dressing gown announcing that he was going to bed and the others could go if they wanted. He then put the models of the Marauder and Mystere under his arm and went upstairs. Hazel just shook her head resignedly and said

that he would be up all night
staring at the models and mut-
tering, then making copious
notes.

Chapter Nine

Beyond Moonrakers

Colin Chapman quickly lost interest in Moonraker itself as it was not his 'baby'. He concentrated on his own boat concept which was to incorporate a modern style with new cutting edge technology - this was the Marauder. Initially there were two potential designs for the Marauder, one designed by Robert Tucker and the other by Don Shead. The project chosen was the Marauder 46, designed by Don Shead (later famous for his designs at Sunseeker) and was first seen at the Earls Court Boat Show in 1973. The Robert Tucker design – by now a half completed wooden prototype was sold on. The Shead designed yellow wooden prototype was actually built for the company by Porter and Haylett of Wroxham. The Marauder was a lovely looking boat, very advanced in technical design and concept. Although 46 foot long with a 14 foot beam, the dry weight was a mere 8 tons (8128kg). The standard engines

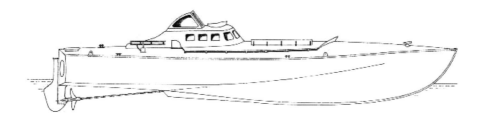

Above: German Klein-Schnellboot WALL II. Note the propeller shaft

were flexibly mounted, 2 turbocharged Ford Sabre 212 BHP diesels. The specification also boasted of the flexibly jointed propeller shafts for the 24" x 27" 4 bladed propellers (it even came with a set of spare propellers as standard).

Colin Chapman was working with performance and speed and when his engineering team were developing the twin skinned VARI system. The power to weight ratio was a key concept in the engineering developments he had his team working on. Colin Chapman was determined that he was going to produce a 46 foot power boat that would undertake 30 knots and so reducing weight and appendage drag was a high priority. The designs on the propeller shaft and rudder however, initially came from the need to prevent drilling holes in the hull at any cost – as any holes were difficult to seal again. With the Marauder,

where a traditional propeller bracket would require fixing was immediately below the fuel tanks – which of course were part of the hull mould. As the Marauder hull was only some 6mm thick (as opposed to the conventionally moulded Moonraker with some 20mm) – any fixings in that position would have to enter the fuel tank.

Once the design team had been tasked with finding an alternative fixing method, it became obvious that they could improve on existing hydrodynamics. As the first 'prototype' Marauder did not have the integrally moulded dual tanks, it had a conventional prop shaft as did the last Marauder built. John Berry knew that the German Navy had developed designs to reduce appendage drag during the Second World War. Therefore he advised Colin Chapman to research this further – but it is very probable that with his knowledge and

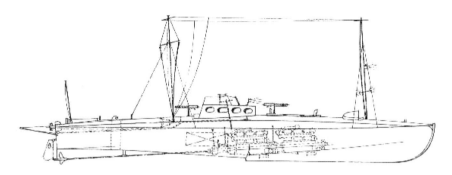

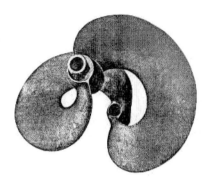

Above: British 55' Thornycroft CMB of 1917. Note reduced extrusions on the propeller shaft mountings.

Right: A British Navy spiral propeller used on the CMB in 1917.

previous research, Colin Chapman was already well aware of these facts . The propshaft with 'P' or 'A' bracket designs along with the rudder was an area Colin Chapman could see room for engineering and design improvement. The traditional brackets cause much appendage drag – about 20% efficiency is lost on the average boat.

Apart from a few sophisticated racing boats, or 1st World War Royal Marine Naval Motor Yachts, no real attention had been focused on the underwater engineering. In fact the Coastal Motor Boats of 1916/7 (for example the 55 foot Thornycroft — named af-

ter Commander Peter Thornycroft who worked on semi-displacement motor yacht designs. He was listed as Number 36 in the 2003 MB&Y most influencial people.) had a spiral propeller remarkably similar to that developed and used by JCL Marine. Like Colin Chapman, the British and German navy were examining all possibilities to improve speed and performance. The Germans had also looked at the propeller and propeller shaft with a view to reducing drag. Their 1944, 10 meter Klein-Schnellboot WAL type I and II demonstrates this. However, they too had problems as the propeller bearings seized up frequently at 2400 revolutions during their early speed trials. This was cured when the bearings were bored to give the shaft another 3mm play – however the loose shaft knocked at lower speeds, although it was fine at higher speeds.

Peter Atkins had been with Moonraker since the early Bell-Buxton days and had risen from what he modestly describes as 'an ordinary boatbuilder' to being in charge of quality control. He undertook the tests with the new propeller shaft design – on the Marauder at that time – and admits to being very apprehensive about such a new design. In fact he fell out with Colin Chapman about this. To improve the efficiency of the underwater performance still further, the initial designs of the Marauder had underwater exhausts which were set forward in the hull and aerated the water to reduce friction drag. Although under water exhausts are now reasonably common place in the racing marine environment, this was a very new concept. However, at the time, they had problems keeping the exhaust noise and vibration down when the boat was not travelling. When the engine was on idle, or the generator in stationary use, the ex-hausts were still needed which not only made an unacceptable level of noise, but rocked the boat from side to side. Therefore, due to the problems with the underwater exhausts, they were only fitted on the first Marauder that was built. On the later models, there was a separate low speed and idle exhaust system which was brought into action at low throttle openings by means of an automatic butterfly valve (also known as 'F' valves).

The exhausts were then diverted through a water damped silencing drum and overboard just above the waterline to avoid the 'tick over engine rumble' which would otherwise arise from conventional exhaust discharge. Diesel engines of the era discharged a lot of smoke and the idea was also to eliminate this nuisance as far as possible.

The engines made as little contact with the hull as possible to reduce the vibration. The engines were suspended on 'space frames' which were hung from the cross members and connected to the main hull using rubber mounts – again to reduce vibration. This initially caused problems, but was eventually resolved successfully. The difficulty was that in practical terms, these frames had to be very, very, precisely placed in each individual boat, otherwise they could not cope with the vibration and they cracked. The Marauder hull however, was designed to flex in the mid section using 'membrane theory'. This allowed the design to absorb the engine vibration without it transmitting to the hull. From the engine, the power went to a universal coupling and this could have had difficulty coping with the thrust of the engines. Again, much money had been spent in design and manufacture. This, Peter Atkins feels, demonstrates how Colin Chapman's drive for a particular project could be seen as a weakness in commercial terms, as he went single mindedly down that path, determined to develop the project at any cost. The attention to detail however was remarkable.

Alan Starkings was responsible for the design of the bilge pump on the Marauder, whereby the mechanism allowed the engines to pump the water out. This particular detail was overseen personally by Colin Chapman himself.

The hull and superstructure was designed to flex, to deal with the pressures and forces upon it. Constant velocity joints had to be used to allow the engine, prop shafts and hull to move without opposing each other – especially as the engines had to be allowed to move independently as they were suspended on the space frames. Still cautious about this new technology, Peter Atkins felt that the initial design was not good enough to stand up to the demands of sea going and had told Colin Chapman that he did not trust the strength of the initial design of the new shaft under thrust. Tony Rudd was the engineer working on the project and had been a friend of Chapman's, joining Lotus in 1969 after success with BRM. He was brought in from Lotus and was a director of both companies. Tony Rudd's excellent engineering skills had found success in the Lotus Formula One team as well as the Lotus car production before working with the marine concepts.

Peter Atkins remembers taking a Marauder down Breydon Water with Colin Chapman standing between the bulkheads, he asked Colin Chapman if he wanted them to go 'flat out' and Colin Chapman replied in the affirmative. This was a test of work in progress and as they increased the speed going up and down the channel in Breydon, Peter Atkins, still cautious, again asked Colin Chapman if he was absolutely sure he wanted full throttle. Peter duly went to full throttle and there was an almighty noise as the prototype prop shaft failed under stress! There are many stories of employees – including management - feeling that Colin Chapman ignored their advice or input when he should have listened. However, much of this advice was based on their gut feelings gained from years of experience, whereas Colin Chapman was trying to use engineering to push forward the boundaries of boat design. His manner was not to argue the point with an employee, instead, he would just walk away, leaving the impression that he was not listening. Some engineers who worked under Colin Chapman have expressed the view that he just had to prove to himself that the designs and ideas that he had carefully worked out in theory, should work in practice. Many state that he was only really interested in forwarding the engineering and the design – the production for sales was often a major inconvenience.

In the final design, the propeller had 4 blades to minimise cyclic thrusts vibrations with a large tip to hull clearance which further reduced vibration transfer to the hull skin. The fuel tanks were located above the propellers to virtually eliminate any vibration transfer. There was no P-bracket, instead there was the special rudder pintle bearing. The rudder design, with a large lateral side area, assisted in reducing the appendage drag even further – this rudder was actually hollow and made from a stainless steel fabrication. The forward propeller shaft bearing was at the hull skin surface and took much of the drive thrust so reducing the thrust load on the engine mountings – allowing the more flexible engine mounting system of 'space frames'. Double universal joints – one of which was a torsionally flexible rubber coupling – eliminated drive alignment problems (which had caused the propeller to come through the bottom of the boat in the early river trials) and also reduced vibration further. The twin disc, down drive gear boxes also allowed level engine installation and yet very small universal joint angles in the drive line. Interestingly enough, this low placement was originally conceived in order to lower the engine as far as possible, which in turn lowered the floor to allow enough height in the passenger accommodation to allow the desired styling. These resultant gear boxes drove the propellers in a contra-rotating manner for balanced drive loads and steering.

The windscreen on the Marauder was also made 'in house'. Due to the large design it was 3 dimensionally convex to ensure that seas ran off it in all directions, rather than a conventional straight surface that could be damaged by heavy seas. Scratch resistant Plexiglass was used – the same as was used on Concorde. It had to be draped over the moulds in order to get the correct shape. It was held in place with rubber mouldings and resins as with the Moonraker screen.

The Marauder was taking a great deal more time to produce than originally planned which was causing problems for the January 1973 Earls Court Boat Show Launch – in fact it was the prototype boat that was actually displayed at the show. The first brochure only included an artist's impression of the boat and the interior shots were taken (again by Stuart White) in a prototype. However, the prototype was good enough to show at the boat show, be taken apart to use to make the moulds and then rebuilt to do the sea trials as the boat had not been evaluated off the drawing board. The second brochure needed photographs of the actual boat and in the November it was only just ready. There was no time to take it to the Mediterranean as planned so, on a cold November Norfolk day, the Marauder was photographed on Breydon Water (the only stretch of the Norfolk Broads you can get up any speed) with models in bikini's on the front. Stuart White remembers using a Moonraker as the photographer's boat, standing on a trestle balanced on the flying bridge to get the height shots Colin Chapman wanted. Apparently, he always had worked out how his boats would be displayed to best advantage and always knew what shots he wanted. They were very lucky that day as the sun really came out, enough to even make the murky grey water on Breydon have a hint of blue. When the photographs were developed Stuart White was pleased with the results, despite the difficulty, as they had to be taken to avoid the navigation posts and the height had hidden the mud flats. He took them to Colin Chapman at Hethel who asked for a magnifying glass. As he poured over the photographs with the magnifying glass Colin Chapman snorted *"Call yourself a photographer – I can see goose bumps on these girls!"*. He was only joking – he too was pleased with the way the very cold shoot had gone. The mock up boat however travelled to the boat show on the back of lorries with men still working on it during the journey.

Colin Chapman had a reputation for working late into the night, his enthusiasm taking over from everything else. He phoned Stuart White up at 9pm on a Sunday night saying he wanted to finish the Marauder brochure and wanted a meeting about it with him and David Lane. Stuart White (who had been half asleep in his chair) said that he would get to Norfolk from his London home early the next day. Colin Chapman announced that he was in David Lane's kitchen and holding the meeting there, David would not leave as his wife was about to give birth. Stuart drove like a mad man to get to Norwich and they had the meeting in David's kitchen well past 1am. At one point the midwife came downstairs and said that David should really go to his wife, Colin Chapman said he couldn't as he was in a meeting. But David went leaving Stuart and Colin Chapman to continue work punctuated with cries as David's daughter was born. Colin Chapman was most surprised that David didn't come back downstairs again for some time!

The first version of the Marauder (Marauder 1) needed 'fine tuning'. Hazel Chapman suggested to her husband that the only way to sort it out was for them to live on the boat themselves for 10 days. They did this in the summer of 1974, after a family holiday they spent 10 days in a little French marina. Although there were strict rules in this marina about not doing your own work on the boat, and not cluttering up the moorings- apparently no-one said anything as the whole mooring pontoon was covered in 'bits of boat' as Colin Chapman and an engineer stripped various parts down. According to Hazel Chapman, the boat returned with a job list of 175 items to change.

Marauder delay

It actually took at least 18 months from the showing of the Marauder at the boat show for the first one to be ready for customer delivery. Although during this time many changes had been made on the Marauder, the delay was in fact a commercial decision. The Marauder had been so well ordered at the 1973 boat show that Colin Chapman decided that it had been priced too low. It was therefore delayed, some changes made in this period and re-launched as the 'Marauder 2' some 18 months later with a higher asking price. This delay did cause some problems however. Leslie Mogford had left the company to work at Jack Powles and when he returned some 18 months later to the Brundall Gardens offices, the yellow wooden prototype Marauder was still outside it with customers still waiting for their actual boats. In fact, he remembers being contacted by a yachting journalist who was asking if the Marauder actually existed or was just a figment of imagination. The Marauder itself was a bit of a mystery to the marine world as having been shown at the boat show, nothing had been seen since, despite a huge interest and so many orders. As it was such innovative technology and production techniques being used, the factory itself was 'top secret' and only those working on the project were allowed clearance to go inside. Colin Chapman also did not want anyone to see the boat until it was perfect – as 'perfection' was a key part of the company image. The

customers who had ordered the boat and paid deposits were, understandably becoming a bit irate by this time at the delays. It was also frustrating for the sales teams waiting for their commission.

Many Marauder sales were converted to Moonraker sales, but one customer became so irate that he had a writ issued for the value of his 'undelivered Marauder'. Moored at Brundall Gardens was a Mystere (a new model, see Page 83) that belonged to a German customer who was awaiting delivery. However, when the Admiralty Marshall arrived – he put the writ for the value of the Marauder on the Mystere which meant that no one was allowed even to get on the boat until the monies were paid and the writ removed. Roy Phillips arrived first on the scene to find the writ on the boat and telephoned the authorities to try and sort matters out on behalf of the German owner. Roy was told that the Admiralty Marshall did not care who owned the boat, but if anybody touched so much as a mooring rope they would be thrown into jail! Eventually, Colin Chapman authorised the payment of the money and the German customer finally got his Mystere!

During the 'delay period', much money was also spent on redesigning the Marauder's interior details. What Colin Chapman had wanted was a complete boat without any fixings on display - he wanted a smooth line and spent thousands of pounds achieving this. There were miles of extrusion scattered around at the yard as designs changed to try and eliminate fittings. Again, great attention to detail was apparent with details such as the fridge. John Standen searched for a supplier of a refrigeration unit and door – and the design team made the fridge to fit the shape of the Marauder hull to maximise available space.

With all the new designs on the Marauder, the boat looked absolutely stunning, but there was still some resistance to the new production methods from within the boat industry. Interestingly enough, one Marauder was especially built for a customer using the hand lay up method rather than resin injection. The customer was a wealthy garage owner who had originally owned a Mamba, unfortunately he later died in a helicopter crash.

Although the VARI produced twin skinned hull was light, there were some initial problems with the strength with the prototypes. Reports of see-

ing prototype boats returning down the river to Brundall with parts of the outer hull skin having crumples, leaving the foam on display have been heard but not verified. As many were very ready to condemn this new moulding system, it is difficult to tell after all this time what is fact and what is exaggeration, especially as any perceived problems were quickly seized upon as proof that the designs did not work. What is known however, is that the first two Marauders did experience some hull problems after hitting objects in the water – one of these was in Germany where Colin Gething was dispatched to oversee the safe return of the vessel and oversee repairs. The second incident happened just off the Yarmouth coast and the owner (understandably) panicked and moored to a navigation buoy until he was rescued and returned to Brundall for repairs. As this incident was transmitted by marine radio, the news travelled like wildfire. Despite these initial teething problems, the VARI technique was developed successfully on all models except the Moonraker and Mamba – although some models were actually produced returning to the hand lay up resin spray methods. JCL claimed that the VARI methods

"..produced strength to weight ratios of around double that achieved by manual hand lay-up processes." In fact the process reduced the weight of the boat by at least half, which enabled them to use much smaller engines to obtain the speed and performance. The design team also experimented with the VARI technique for coffins – until it was realised that they could not be safely burnt – and also for moulding luxury baths on behalf of a large manufacturer.

Leslie Mogford remembers going out for the first time on a Marauder with Tony Rudd and John Standen from Technocraft. They took the boat down to Breydon water – at a speed of about 12 knots they hit the side of the mud flat channel. Leslie Mogford rushed to the engine room to check the mud in the filters – he had not seen the boat apart from the prototype as it was still so 'top secret'. He could not believe that the water pump filters were plastic (so saving weight) and said so, pointing out the danger of melting if the engine over heated and a resulting fire. The reply was to the effect that the last thing you'd worry about is the water pump filter melting if you were in that situation. The filters were full of Norfolk Broad mud and Leslie was looking for something to use to get it out of the filters. But as the boat had not been through the marketing department, it had no 'kit', not even a mop. In the end the men had to dismantle the aerial to use this to poke the mud out of the filters before re-starting the engine. They were all a bit apprehensive that Colin Chapman would get to hear that they had 'crashed the boat' on its first proper outing. Despite any fears that some had for the strength of this new type of hull for easily damaging, there was no damage from impact on the mud flat even at this speed.

As well as being driven to reduce vibration, Colin Chapman also wanted to reduce the noise of the boat so that people could travel in comfort. Despite the Lloyds certificate and improvements, the Moonraker was still a relatively noisy boat, to the extent that when Doug Brixton, one of the Lloyds inspectors came to take the Moonraker out, he insisted on wearing ear defenders for the sea trials. In comparison, in the Marauder, people sat in the cockpit could hold a conversation while travelling at some speed. All mechanical and potentially noise generating machinery were located in a fully sound proofed 'systems bay' located under the main saloon and bridge deck. It was accessed through a sound proofed hatch off the forward companion way. One of Colin Chapman's tests for noise on the Marauder was to release a smoke bomb in the engine compartment to test that the seals were working. The theory behind this was that if smoke could get through the seals and escape the engine compartment, then so could noise.

The design of the Marauder had learnt from the 'wet ride' lessons of the Moonraker and the careful location of the spray rails, along with the hull design, gave a comparatively 'dry' ride even in heavy seas. The sales teams technical brochure boasted that the Marauder had *"....displayed the highest operating propulsive efficiency and the highest lift/drag ration of any known luxury motor yacht."*

The Marauder and Marauder Two were initially well ordered by customers. In January 1976, they obtained about £750,000 of combined orders for the Marauder and Mystere at the Earls Court boat show. There was undoubtedly some lost sales due to the commercially delayed production – and maybe a few from the (arguably

unfair) reputation it acquired within the marine industry as being unreliable in heavy seas as the first couple sold had returned with problems. These initial problems were fixed to satisfaction. However, what arguably really affected the sales was the fact that by the time the Marauder was finally actually produced, the Mystere was in production. The Italian styling of this boat captured the eye and the Marauder paled in comparison. Some believe that details such as the windows looked dated by the time it was in production. Although not as many Marauders were sold as Moonrakers, there are still some in existence today and they fetch good money on the second hand boat market. By April 1979 the records show that 10 Marauders had been completed and sold.

Mystere

By 1975, JCL were concentrating on a new range of Italian designed boats aimed at the Mediterranean market - the Mystere, Mirage, and Mamba. Colin Chapman had long admired the Italian design and had studied the way the Italian's

Above: Mystere photographed at speed on Breydon Water

were building. The Mystere was built from an Italian wooden hulled boat originally designed by Antonio Maggini in 1972, under licence. Versilcraft of Viareggio had been producing the hull for 2 years. Initially, the agreement was that JCL were going to develop the VARI technique for this vessel and then Versilcraft were going to produce it under licence. However, it was decided that JCL would continue to produce the Mystere in the UK. From the original boat, moulds were made to manufacture the boat in fibreglass. A mould had to be taken from the wooden craft – although this was relatively simple for the hull, Maggini's superstructure design with many reverse curves made the superstructure moulding very complex having to be in several sections. The VARI technique therefore was only used for the hull, not the superstructure. The original wooden boat was sold by Roy Phillips to an English customer on the south coast.

The Mystere, launched in 1975 was 43 feet long and had 4 permanent berths with the emphasis on space – and was definitely aimed at the export market as it was more usual for 6+ berths on a boat of this size to appeal to the domestic market (North Sea). The initial version was fitted with twin Perkins TV8 510M turbo-charged V8's, each producing 235 bhp - housed beneath the saloon. For the 1976 Earl's Court Boat Show there was an engine option offered of Sabre 210 hp straight 6 turbo-charged which were repositioned beneath the cockpit, driving the propellers through 'v' boxes. Although there was no change in the performance, there was a reduction in fuel consumption with this option and this option cost £5,000 less. The engines were mounted on specially designed GFRP engine beds that carried soft rubber mountings which absorbed the vibration and resonance. This prevented its transmission through the craft's structure. The flexible engine exhaust passed through the topsides to the external exhaust boxes and so allowed the expansion of hot gases to take place outside. This further reduced the running noise. The optional ONAN 6 KVA generator was also fully contained within its own sound shield and the engine room was sound insulated. The fixed interior furniture was made in wood with a sprayed paint finish which was so good that it was often mistaken for fibreglass.

The Mystere was built under the patented VARI system with a Lloyds' certificate and boat reports in specialist magazines admired the handling and engineering. One 1975 report in Motor Boat and Yachting thought it rather expensive – a basic version in 1975 priced at £62,300 ex VAT - but acknowledged that it was suited to the export market. This report highlighted the plus points of the Mystere were:

- good seakeeping qualities
- well engineered
- exceptional internal trim
- revolutionary hull construction
- large saloon and living area.

The report found that the weak points of the Mystere were:

- single fuel tank
- poor stern visibility at helm
- awkward galley layout
- few superstructure grab rails
- little interior ventilation.

The Mystere – along with the other 'Mediterranean models' had almost all Italian produced fittings from the windows to the light fittings. Colin Chapman had continued to admire the design of Italian manufacture as opposed to the functionality of the British counterparts. Great thought had also gone into how the decks were constructed. On both the Mystere and the Mirage the wooden decks look thick. In fact they are only a few millimetres thick – the wooden covering was vacuumed onto a beamed structure that was placed in the corrugated deck moulding. The result was a very strong structure that was also very light and the same principle was used in the flying bridge construction. This system is commonplace in marine manufacture today.

Mystere boat shows

The Hamburg boat show was the first one where JCL had to display the boats outside on hard standing. It was in an industrial area and it was very difficult to keep the boat clean. It was easier to send someone back to Hethel to collect plastic sheeting and bring it back to Hamburg than buy plastic sheeting in Hamburg itself. The sheeting was used to build a canopy to protect the boat and also to disguise the unattractive wall it was placed next to. The show did not go well – morale was low amongst the sales team to the extent that when Leslie Mogford had to leave the show to book the Amsterdam Hiswa

show, on his return 48 hours later, the sales team had left. This was unheard of in the company. At the end of the show, the Mystere was put back in the water ready for the return journey to prepare it for its customer.

They moved the boat to Wedel Marina, but on the way hit an object in the water which damaged the propellers. This incident happened due to the visibility through the windscreen – due to the ride of the boat you had a blind spot for approximately 60 feet in front of the bow. If not using the flybridge, it was common practice to use the radar to detect movement of craft while manoeuvring on rivers etc. Anecdotal evidence tells of when demonstrating the boat to customers, they only did it when the sun was shining to encourage use of the exterior and, even then, having an employee outside keeping a look out as forward visibility was so poor from the interior wheel position. Paul Pardon came out with Don Smythe to fix the mechanical problems (coincidentally, in approximately 2000, Don met a Marauder owner in Turkey – he was still delighted with his boat and even more so that Don was able to fix a couple of small problems. Sadly, Don died in

2002).

The whole episode does illustrate some of the impracticality of the Mystere (a catchphrase of Colin Chapman himself was "the glorious impracticality of the Mystere") not only the blind spot from the interior helm position, but also in the problems they had repairing the damage. Ideally to fix the propellers, the boat should have been fully lifted out of the water. However, due to the complex hull moulding, it needed its special lifting cradle which used the locator on the water inlets in the hull moulding. Colin Chapman had envisaged that each boat would be sold with a cradle, but this never came into being. Therefore to mend the propellers, they took the risk of using a huge cradle with conventional slings on a slipway, with the boat stern first. They only lifted the stern slightly out of the water, leaving the midships and bow in. As they had everything ready for changing the propellers, the job was completed in about fifteen minutes and the boat returned into the water with no further harm.

Fiskhavan 1976

This has been described as the 'boat show from hell' which was held in the red light district of Hamburg during an export drive to the German market. During the boat show itself, for safety reasons the boat had to be empty of fuel, but as the Mystere was to be transported under its own steam from the show, obviously it needed to be fuelled up. Fuel barges patrolled the river in order to fill commercial vessels with fuel and the Mystere was taken to one of these for re-fuelling. Such was the size of the re-fuelling barge that the Mystere was some 60 feet below its deck. An order for fuel was shouted up to the barge – but unfortunately the amount got mistranslated and instead of 1000 litres, approximately 10 tonnes was ordered. Even more unfortunately, the barge was fitted with an extremely fast and highly pressurised industrial fuel delivery system which pumped in fuel quicker than the air could escape from the fuel tank. This popped off the neoprene gasket with the moulded in pipes and jubilee clips attached to the one central fuel tank. The bilge and forward accommodation was full of fuel - and the Mystere was lined with marcasite !

The sales team managed to pump out the fuel from the boat interior and easily replace the gasket and jubilee clips, but were left with a rather smelly boat to return to a satisfactory state to deliver to a customer before they returned home. Again in Wedel marina, the team scrubbed the boat with industrial cleaner and left the carpets out on the walls to dry – all to no avail – the smell stubbornly remained. In the end Roger Putnam came over from Hethel and brought a large bottle of duty free Chanel No 5 perfume which was applied liberally. It took about 14 days, but the boat was eventually transferred to a satisfied customer – which pleased the team no end as they had all wanted to be home with their families for November 5th.

Dusseldorf, February 1977

The following February saw the Mystere being taken to Dusseldorf in a continuation of the German sales drive. This show was notable for the appalling weather – there had been floods in Brundall, which had flooded Brundall Gardens offices. This included the office where the carpet tiles that were used to cover the boat show stand were stored. The wet tiles were loaded in a van, Roger Putnam and Brian Perks travelled to the show via Felixstowe and Leslie Mogford went via Harwich. The boat was being taken by sea and was severely delayed by the bad weather. For the crew travelling with the van and tiles, the weather was so bad that by Arnhem it had begun to snow, the temperature dropped and the windscreen wipers froze – as did the wet floor tiles in the back of the van.

Dusseldorf was 12 degrees below freezing – as was the reception the sales team received from the event organisers when the news of the Mystere delay was broken. They were told in no uncertain terms that if the boat was not in the hall by 12 midday on Saturday, it would not be allowed in. The show itself opened on the Monday morning and the Italian exhibitors were already protesting about the late arrival of the Mystere – they certainly didn't want the competition.

In the meantime, there had been no sign of the Mystere, eventually the German river police found it having some technical difficulties and assisted its progress to the hall after some financial persuasion.

Leslie Mogford managed to use the same persuasion to get security to "open the doors" on the Sunday morning so they could get the boat in. The boat was filthy with industrial pollution and covered in snow and ice after the journey – as it was icy outside, the team had been unable to wash the boat before it entered the show hall.

However, having got the doors open, another obstacle stood in the way. The crane operator thought the boat was too heavy for his equipment – it actually was, but the team blatantly fibbed about the weight. While the rest of the team kept the crane operator talking, it is alleged that Roger Putnam undid the crane's fuse box and disconnected the circuit breaker to ensure the boat got lifted in position. The boats already in place in the hall were immaculate and in show condition when the wet and filthy Mystere was lifted over them into position. Sheets of black snow fell off and landed on competitors' boats – much to the outrage of their sales teams, especially a Possilippo.

The team worked all day and night to clean the boat and build the stand – but the final disaster happened when Leslie Mogford hurriedly drove the Luton van full of equipment into the hall, dodging the organisers. He had forgotten about the height of the van cab - and the overhang of a bow of a 50 foot 'Hattaras European' that stood between the hall entrance and the Mystere stand he was heading for. The inevitable collision punched a 2 foot hole in the bow and the force actually moved the boat across its stand. As the rows broke out, John Newman quickly jumped in the Luton van and whisked it out of sight while the rest of the team dragged the still frozen floor tiles in a heap to defrost. Somehow Roger Putnam, who had a reputation as being able to smooth any problem out – lived up to this and pacified the 'Hattaras' team. Such were his skills that they even consented to putting the 'For Sale' sign to cover the hole made by the Luton van !

Corsica 1977

Paul Pardon (sales and service side) whom Colin Chapman nicknamed the 'company holidaymaker' as he was abroad for most of the time - was stuck in Corsica for 8 days in 1977 with a boat whose gear box had failed. Paul couldn't get off the island as there was great trouble with the Partisans fighting and civil unrest on Corsica at that time – all flights were cancelled. Paul actually got shot in the leg while trying to get into town to phone for help. All the phones were out as all the kiosks had been blown up, any calls had to be made from the local post office – queues for the post office went right around the block. The post office also had erratic opening (or more often closed) times. While trying to get into town to place a call back to the UK to let the company know what was going on and get a replacement gearbox, Paul ran into a local skirmish. Despite keeping his head down, a bullet ricocheted off a wall resulting on a flesh wound to his left thigh – Paul just applied antiseptic cream and has suffered little more than a small scar! Much of the troubles were not visible from the harbour, but a very good view was had of the seaplanes swooping into the sea to scoop up water to dump in the mountains to flush the terrorists out. After a couple of unsuccessful days at the post office, Paul found his way to what looked like a wooden hut – it was in fact the local yacht club. They had a phone, but initially would not let Paul

use it, but after consuming 3 very large scotch and American Dry's Paul was allowed to phone for help. As his speech was affected by the alcohol, the yard initially thought it was a drunken prank – but eventually were persuaded to send out a gearbox on the first flight able to get into Corsica. Paul duly arranged for the gearbox to be installed and fled back to the safety of Cannes.

Mirage

The Mirage introduced in 1977 used the Mystere hull but with a very different layout and superstructure. Part of the deal with Versilcraft was that JCL retained the right to use the 'Mystere' hull. As the JCL/ Technocraft team designed this superstructure and layout, they ensured that it had no reverse angles for ease of mouldings. The use of space was optimised when compared to the Maggini interior – as the new interior had 6 as opposed to 4 berths and 2 bathrooms. A long term contract was announced in 1977 for 5 Mirage during 1978-9 for Interplan Yachting which was estimated to be worth £250,000. The Mirage was 43 foot long with a 14.2 foot beam

Above: Mirage at speed

Below: Mamba at speed

and a dry weight of 7.36 tons. It had accommodation for 6 + 2 guests plus one crew and could exceed 26 knots, powered by 2, flexibly mounted turbocharged Ford Sabre 212 bhp diesel engines. The propellers (18" x 18") were mounted on universally jointed propeller shafts. This contract fell into difficulties and only one or two of the boats were ever delivered and paid for.

Mamba

The Mamba, introduced in 1976 was a smaller version of the Mirage and was also launched as the Mamba 'Plus Two' at the 1979 Earls Court boat show at a cost of £82,000. The 'Plus Two' version had a different front cabin layout, with a double berth rather than 2 singles and was really just a marketing ploy in an attempt to improve sales. The Mamba was a 4 berth, 37.6 foot long with a beam of 14.2 foot and a dry weight of 4.93 tons, It was powered by two, flexibly mounted turbocharged Mercraft 180 bhp diesel engines with universally jointed propeller shafts to 17" x 19" three bladed propellers. Interestingly, the Mirage and Mamba had 'P' brackets made of manganese bronze and, like the other models, they were provided with a pair of spare propeller shafts and propellers.

Although much of the main development and engineering advancements had been made with the Marauder – the design team were constantly striving to find better ways to do things. With the Mamba, they experimented with extending their success in 'honeycomb' bulkhead moulding to the floor. The bulkheads were extremely strong despite being only 6mm thick - they were pre stressed when placed in the moulding channels. Cosmetic padding was used where it was needed to make them look thicker. In fact the hull and superstructure moulding had become so advanced, that it was now possible to construct the interior of the boat and place it in one piece into the locating channels of the hull moulding. However, when the honeycombed moulding process was used on the first Mamba floor – it proved not to be so successful. During a trial on Breydon the boat crossed the wash of another vessel. As the Mamba bounced across the rough water, the passengers also bounced – and landed straight through the floor !

The Mamba was also featured in conjunction with the Martini adverts of the time. Martini even ran a competition with the top prize being a special edition of the Mamba called the 'Streaker'. This had the conventional hull but with a wooden superstructure. This, sadly was won by a man who had no interest in a boat and for a while it remained in limbo at Brundall Gardens. Eventually the owner insisted that the boat was sold on his behalf. Roy Phillips sold it to a customer in Geneva and the boat was used on the lake in Switzerland. The design team used the concepts from this 'one off' superstructure to develop a project intended to rival the Italian 'Riva' – these used the Mamba hull, but were very futuristically designed. Unfortunately, this project did not develop beyond the design stage.

At about this time, John Player were sponsoring Colin Chapman's Formula One team with the now famous black and gold livery. They were also sponsoring Tom Percival who was a successful speed boat racer. Colin Chapman became interested in power boat racing and for a while his son, Clive very successfully competed in power boat races on Oulton Broad. It was during this time that John Player organised an event to make the most of the fact that they were sponsoring the top team in Formula One car racing and the World Power Boat Champion. They had Tom Percival in his power boat pitched against with Emerson Fittipaldi in his Lotus to see who would be the first to reach 100 mph

There were also discussions regarding the possibility of Colin Chapman re-designing the Mamba for Percival's racing, but unfortunately Tom Percival was killed before this could progress further. Approximately seven Mamba were built and delivered to customers.

Mistral

This was a special version of the Mirage which had been designed in 1978 especially to meet the very high specification of an American organisation who had wanted twelve craft to an American standard. This included bigger beds, modified toilet system, American capacity fridge and freezer provision and many specific interior details such as

Above: The Mirage featured high quality interiors to meet the requirements of discerning customers, including a member of the Jordanian Royal Family. The Mistral was designed as a special version of the Mirage, specifically for the American market and it was hoped that this would become the basis of future business with Chris-Craft International Inc. The failure to secure this business contributed to the eventual failure of Colin Chapman's boat business.

curtains. A marine designer of some repute in the USA, John Bannenberg, was used to design the interior. This was with the intent of appealing to the American market as discussions with Chris-Craft were progressing in this area. John Bannenberg was used to working on super yachts of 120 feet and the QE2. The potential American buyers, Chris-Craft International Inc., had also ordered tests on the noise and vibration produced. Unfortunately, despite all the work carried out, this deal eventually fell through, mainly due to the fact that Chris-Craft kept changing the specification they wanted.

They wanted these boats and the twelve Mamba's they had also ordered to meet the US Coastguard requirements and their list of specifications kept increasing and changing. Eventually Colin Chapman lost patience with this. The collapse of these negotiations and resultant lost sale, contributed to the eventual company liquidation.

A special version of the Mirage was also commissioned for a close relative of King Hussein of Jordan. This cost £165,000 and included two large fish freezing compartments, which replaced the crew accommodation in the bow. This boat also had Volvo in-

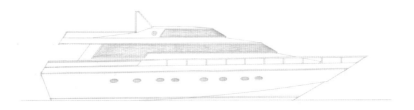

Above: This 17.5 metre design was one of a number of designs from the closing period of JCL Marine. It demonstrates the range of styles under consideration. In this period one of the major opportunities was the hoped for link with Chris-Craft.

board mounted outboard engines fitted instead the standard engine provision. This was to enable the vessel to operate in very shallow waters. The surviving records of April 1979 show that six Mystere had been sold, twelve Mirage and seven Mamba.

Mangusta

This was a 65 foot boat, which was designed by JCL team with a good deal of input from Chapman himself. It had originated from a 58 foot concept, ordered by Chris-craft to be designed and built by JCL Marine on 25th November 1976.

This order was never fulfilled, as the whole negotiations with Chris-Craft fell through. However, Colin Gething undertook all the drawings for this and the 65 foot version, but these were only general drawings of the hull and detail of the superstructure. It had not been tank tested, or progressed beyond the wooden mock up model within JCL before liquidation.

Above: The Moonraker 36 was a popular model and seven were on order for the very competitive Dutch market in 1974.

Chapter Ten

Dealing with the problems facing the boat industry

By the end of 1975, the UK boat industry was hitting a slump, due to the effects of 25% VAT applied to boats and a massive slump in the domestic market gripped by inflation and recession. JCL however were comparatively well off as, by 1974, between 50-75% of sales were to the export market. The Moonraker was particularly attractive to the foreign market despite being targeted by the companies' non-Moonraker products. In August 1974, they had broken into the highly competitive Dutch market when they received a £180,000 order for seven Moonraker 36's. This order was handled by the Dutch distributor Van Dorst Yachting, operated by Rene Van Dorst, owner of one of the country's leading garage concerns.

In June that year a Moonraker had been sold to the Minister of Defence of Bahrein, Sheik Bin Eissa Al-Khalifa. He named his boat 'Bandar' in a deep yellow colour with the extras costing nearly as much as in 1978, to put boats on display on the back of trucks in and around London. 1978 had been rather a static year in terms of boat sales and it was with some relief that in September, JCL were able to announce orders of just over one million pounds. This included a commission to design a personal version of the Mirage for Prince Abdulla Masood of Abu Dhabi which had followed a visit by a party of nine, representing the Prince, to the boat show.

In January 1979, again saw the launch of another export drive to improve sales at the Earls Court and Dusseldorf boat shows. At Earls Court, they were showing the Mirage and the Moonraker F/350, whereas in Germany they were showing the Marauder Two, the Mirage, the Moonraker F/350 and the Mamba 'Plus Two'. They also decided to sell direct to the German market rather than through agents as previously and in March 1979 employed a German Market Liaison Officer – Valerie Minkley. She was responsible for co-ordinating the firm's marketing activities in Germany, Switzerland and Austria. By eliminating the 25% discount the agents had demanded, the company hoped to be more competitive in 1979, providing that the relationship between the pound and DM did not worsen and so negate any benefit.

The market had also changed – the Northern European market's interest had moved back towards motor sailing vessels. Despite cosmetically updating the Moonraker, the sales of this previously very popular model dropped. The main opportunities appeared to be in the Middle East, which was where the company was aiming its Mediterranean models.

In April 1979, JCL displayed £350,000 worth of yachts close to Yarmouth Haven Bridge. The marketing team had invited 40 overseas visitors and 35 local couples to inspect the vessels and go on sea trials in an attempt to boost sales. The Marauder (now costing £150,000) was not on display, the reason being given was that all the completed models had been sold and delivered. However, on display were a

Moonraker (priced at £50,000), a Mamba (£55,000) and a Mirage (£125,000). They were to be joined by a Mystere (£120,000). The Moonraker nearly didn't make the journey up from Brundall as it struck an underwater object en route – it was repaired in time for the display after builders worked through the night.

However, under the glossy public relations spin, there was evidence that problems were starting to affect JCL. By this time there was a steady loss of staff, including Roger Putnam who returned to Lotus Cars. At the Yarmouth display, Mr Graham Arnold announced a rationalisation programme for the company which would take place over Easter. After this date, all laminated glass-fibre work would be carried out at the Hethel plant, whereas all fitting out of the hulls would be undertaken at Brundall. It was estimated that this would save £450 per vessel built. Some thought had to be taken regarding the logistics of transporting the hulls between the sites. A trailer could take the one and a half tonne hull from Hethel to Brundall, whereas transporting the finished boat, which could weigh up to 9 tonnes, required expensive, specialist haulage firms.

This change of working did have an impact on the forty nine staff at Hethel, at the time the company employed 165 in total, a reduction from the 170+ employed the year before). Only 13 of these Hethel-based staff were laminators who therefore would not be affected. Amongst the other 36, there were 16 who did not want to move to Brundall due to the travelling. They were to be offered positions at Lotus Cars. The transport of hulls was not to be without its hazards and, on the 10th April 1979, an empty Mirage hull slipped from its cradle on the Heartsease roundabout in Norwich on its way from Hethel to Brundall.

Some report that the 'cracks' in the company had started to show earlier than this. Although everybody interviewed by the author said how much they enjoyed working at Moonraker/JCL because it was so vibrant and interesting, some have also spoken of how morale changed in the period before liquidation. There was some jealousy of those staff who moved to what was seen as the 'posh' Brundall Gardens offices from those staying in their floating houseboat offices, although the two sites were not far apart. The further split to the Hethel site added to this feeling amongst staff and some feel that it added to the difficulties due to the distance between the sites – the roads in Norfolk were not as good as today making the journey time relatively long for the actual distance travelled. Two definite 'camps' appeared to emerge from this: 'Moonraker' and 'JCL'. An air of uncertainly during this late period of the company's history is described by many former employees, and it was noticeable that staff either left to work for competitors, or returned to Lotus Cars. It also became apparent that Colin Chapman's interest in the company had waned and, due to his charismatic personality, this affected everything. As sales dropped, those on commission-only payments were often in financial hardship and had to find other work. Anecdotes from the final year, tell of when a customer did call in at the factory, of how they were introduced to as many sales people as possible and the visit arranged around lunch time. This was so that more than one sales person could legitimately take the customer to lunch at the Yare Pub 'on expenses'.

The company had also obtained a reputation for paying its bills late - this may have been rather unfair. In the motor trade it was common business practice to have a 90 day credit period. This was not the same in the marine industry, but it would appear that it was only when the industry hit difficult times that suppliers complained about Moonraker/JCL's 90 day payment practice.

One example of this was at a Southampton boat show. A supplier whose bill remained unpaid waited until a boat show for maximum effect and took this opportunity to serve a writ. This writ was plastered all over the display Moonraker. It meant that no one could go near the boat and even worse, it was very obvious and rather embarrassing to the company image. Colin Chapman was reportedly furious, but it did have the desired effect of getting the bill paid very quickly so the writ could be removed.

In September 1979, JCL were reported by the local press to be experiencing problems with their sales, due to the rising value of the pound, plus raw material price increases due to the UK inflation. The firm, however continued its pressure on the export market. At the Southampton boat show, they used the latest versions of the Mirage (£143,000) and Moonraker (£63,000) to take a

group of leading foreign yachting journalists to the Isle of
Wight and back for dinner.

Above: Lotus 79. For many, Colin Chapman is synonymous with the Lotus racing cars, and particularly for the black painted John Player Specials sponsored by the John Player tobacco company. Technological innovation was exchanged both ways between the racing car development and the boat development.

Chapter Eleven

JCL /Moonraker and it's relationship with Lotus Cars

Although commercially and legally separate companies, they in fact worked very closely. Behind them both was the driving force of Colin Chapman himself whose charisma and energy in design and enterprise had immense impact, shaping the direction of the companies. One of the main marine production sheds was for a while on the Hethel site where all the production using the VARI techniques was undertaken. Of course, some of the technology was the same and so there was sharing of technological advances and developments through Technocraft Ltd., especially the VARI and adhesive bonding process. Technocraft served as the research and development company for both the car and marine production companies. VARI after all, had emerged out of the car production process and was used on all Lotus car bodies up until the Elise model. The last Esprit produced used the VARI process, as had the Excel (Eclat) and Elite. The transfer of the VARI patents from Group Lotus to Technocraft had been on the 11th February 1977, when the VARI patent had also been assigned. Lotus had then bought the rights to the non-marine VARI patents and, after liquidation, bought the non-automotive VARI rights in 1985.

Both companies were organised in a similar fashion, both in terms of production and management. Much of this is not surprising as many of the key personnel like Warren King, Tony Rudd and Fred Bushell worked for both companies. Sales teams moved from one to another with similar ease and Stuart White undertook the photography and promotions for both companies, as did Ron Middleton of Focalpoint.

There were the same pressures on both companies in terms of space. At one point Warren King had overseen the purchase of a Ludham company who produced waterbeds and light fittings. The only reason they wanted this company was because it had the right planning permissions for business use and large, new production sheds. The company fulfilled it's existing orders for waterbeds and light fittings, it was intended to use the sheds for marine production, but in the end it was used for the stainless steel production and for car manufacture from about 1977, in fact the Sunbeam Lotus was produced from there. The site was eventually sold to Moores of Wroxham in 1984.

After the James Bond movie 'Moonraker' in 1979, there was one boat show that had a stand with both the Moonraker and the Lotus Esprit on it, the Lotus having been featured in the Bond film. There was also a submarine moored at the quay to give added interest for potential customers. Arguably, they were both targeting the same market, that is the luxury end and so the marketing activities were very similar, just a different product.

They were also supposedly able to combine forces in July 1979 when postal problems were causing mail to the continent being delayed for two weeks or more. This was having an effect on export business throughout the UK. According to a local press report, to solve the problem, a Moonraker took Lotus Cars' and JCL Marine's post from Yarmouth to Ijmuiden in Holland, from there the post allegedly entered the European postal service and avoided the delays. This jour-

Above: Brigadier General James "Jimmy" Stewart. Hethel was home to the 389th Bombardment Wing 'the Stars Wing' of the US 8th Army Air Force during WWII. Flying B24 Liberators commanded by James Stewart and including a number of Hollywood actors and writers. The Marauder was initially built where Jimmy Stewart's B24 had once been serviced.

ney in fact did not take place, once the press had their story and had taken their photographs of a Moonraker departing Yarmouth, when the coast was clear, the Moonraker in fact turned back to the UK. Another coup for the marketing department for both Moonraker/JCL and Lotus Cars!

Criticisms have been levelled at Colin Chapman's over riding interest in the engineering design, in both his car

Above: Where once the mighty B24 Liberators of the 389th Bom-bardment Wing were serviced, a line of Colin Chapman's boats await shipment to their new owners.

and marine concerns. This interest, the critics believe, over rode the economic concerns for viable production costs for a product to sell the consumers.

Above: A model of the microlight aircraft which was Chapman's latest interest.

Chapter Twelve

Final days of JCL

Mario Andretti, the Lotus F1 World Champion, summed up the strength and weakness of Colin Chapman

" He could pull the best ideas from everyone. There is the misconception that he was the One sole genius but he in fact extracted ideas from all around making what were to be the final decisions. He had an absolute craving for ideas.."

"When he was distracted, as at one time he was by his boat-building business, the Team suffered tremendously. After Long Beach in 1976, Chapman was somewhat down, and at breakfast I said to him that if he gave 100%, and let the boats go

105

to someone else, I would give 100%."

By 1980, Colin Chapman was bored by the marine industry, just as he was bored with the road car production. He was at this time, and just before his sudden death, very interested in diversifying into small aircraft production, particularly microlights which at this time were unregulated in the UK, and he thought had great potential for engineering design and development. He thought that with the potential future problems with traffic and road congestion in the UK that microlights could be used as small planes were used in the USA. To this end Colin Gething worked on design and construction changes to an existing canard type solid winged enclosed model by Bert Rutan. Roger Pestell and Bob Cornish both worked at Ketteringham Hall producing these changes. This adapted model was then to have been produced and sold by the original manufacturer.

Hazel Chapman offers a great insight into her husband's psyche when she explains why, out of all his enterprises, he best loved the Formula One racing. This explanation probably explains why the car and marine production businesses had such problems and why he

has been greatly criticised for this. Colin Chapman loved the challenge of solving a problem and, with Formula One, you had the winter to develop the new car, within a set of known guidelines. In the spring, it was tested and any problems immediately worked on, as you were only using two or three cars. By March you were racing the car, and again any problems could be approached immediately. It was this immediacy that held Colin Chapman's attention. Both with the road cars and boats, there would be a huge delay between a technical solution, or development, and production. Then, there would be the customers who would complain and Colin Chapman had no patience with this. Once he or his team had finished a design, or solved a problem, that was it as far as he was concerned, and his brain and interest had moved on to the next project. It was almost as if once he lost the personal control of the project, often through it becoming too big an enterprise, problems developed and he lost interest.

By the beginning of 1980, the previously strong export sales began to drop off and JCL/Moonraker finally started to suffer with the economic climate and had to downsize production with resultant job losses. With high inflation and virtually no domestic market to speak of, it was a bleak time for the UK boat industry as a whole. Many other boat builders had either gone out of business, or downsized their operations.

Within JCL, much time had been spent in negotiation with the American company Chris-Craft, and its principal Herbie Siegel, regarding the Mistral and Mamba. Tony Rudd and Jim Rochlis were very involved with these negotiations that appeared promising despite being very protracted, unfortunately it all came to nothing. This was a major blow as this major contract had been for design and build of two boats, a 24 foot craft and mould tools, as well as the 58 foot Mangusta, combined with a total order for twenty four other models. It was also anticipated that the entry onto the American market would result in many orders, and cash generation from the licence agreements. It would appear that Chris-Craft's main goal was to acquire the rights to use the VARI technique in the USA and indeed a licence agreement was signed on 26th November 1976 for Chris-Craft to acquire the VARI licence and 'know how' from JCL Marine and Technocraft. Chris-Craft also wanted the distribution rights to the Mamba, Mistral, Mystere, Marauder and Moonraker and signed an agreement to this affect, also on the 26th November 1976. This early date of '1976' demonstrates how protracted the negotiations were. The original order from Chris-Craft to JCL Marine for twelve Mistral was placed on 25th November 1976, and twelve Mamba placed on the 16th December 1976. Eventually both parties withdrew from the negotiations and Chris-Craft ended up with their parent company being taken over as part of the Time Warner organisation.

Cancelled export orders in 1978 had added to already difficult circumstances. Over the winter of 1979 there had been a lack of firm orders and no forward cash flow to fund production. The numerous sales prospects failed to be turned into orders due to the financial climate of high interest rates and the export market was badly affected by the strong pound.

Gordon Reed had been lured from competitor Jack Powles in 1979 in an attempt to use his knowledge of the Eastern Markets. He and Martin Church had taken all the boat models to the Singapore boat show and from there to Hong Kong in a last ditch attempt to obtain orders. Inchcape had expressed interest and much time and effort was spent in negotiating a deal. Both Gordon and Martin had returned from Hong Kong convinced that they had a deal and for a few days there appeared to be light at the end of a rather bleak tunnel.

The final curtain came with the loss of this £1.25 million order from Inchcape, Hong Kong for eight boats. Apparently there had been some problems over time scales and delivery that were insurmountable. The business was so fragile that the next day, the board members had met at lunch time and decided that the only option was voluntary liquidation. The employees were told the same day at 14:30 hrs. The wages had been paid in cash rather than the usual cheque, perhaps an indication of the precarious state of affairs.

On the 31st October 1980 JCL Marine Ltd, Moonraker Motor Yachts and Marauder Ltd went into voluntary liquidation. Moonraker Marine International Ltd had been 'wound up' earlier after Versilcraft negotiations. By now, there were only 70 employees who all lost their jobs and en-tered a very bleak employment market. In a newspaper interview, Tim Enright stressed that there was no connection between Lotus Cars and JCL/Moonraker despite the fact that four directors of JCL/Moonraker companies were also directors of Lotus Cars, Colin Chapman was Chairman of Lotus Cars and a director of JCL, along with Fred Bushell, Tim Enright and Tony Rudd. Moonraker Motor Yachts had Fred Bushell and Tim Enright as Directors.

Donald Draper and John Morel of Kidsons, chartered accountants, were appointed joint liquidators by the creditors. Later that month, creditors were told that JCL Marine had a deficit of nearly £1 million when they went into liquidation. This was actually split £965,000 to JCL Marine Ltd and £465,000 to Moonraker Motor Yachts Ltd. The accountants estimated that in reality the combined deficit did not add up because some creditors' claims were duplicated in the liquidations.

While JCL and Moonraker were liquidated in 1980, the development and research company Technocraft Ltd remained. Technocraft became 'Hethel Engineering Ltd' in approximately 1985. The situation, to some extent mirrored the situation with Lotus Cars. When General Motors took over Lotus, they initially wanted to cease production of the road car and just keep the research and development branch, as it was the development and sale of technical solutions that was financially viable. Luckily for the lover of Lotus Cars, they were persuaded that the road car was the best advert of their technical expertise.

Colin Chapman died suddenly of a heart attack in December 1982.

Why did Moonraker/JCL fail?

One of the most common explanations of why this, previously highly successful, company was suddenly forced into liquidation is often laid at the door of the economic climate, combined with a sudden loss of large orders and the massive impact of VAT on boat prices.

These factors undoubtedly had their part to play, but are not the only reasons. Competition from other UK companies was by now very strong as compared to the early 1970's, with Fairline, Powles and Princess all fighting for the narrowing market share. The years of high development costs had also starved the company of available money as the resultant sales, despite the buoyant press release statements, were not as good as hoped and so had not recouped these costs. In the final year there are many tales of trying to place orders with suppliers who were wary of giving credit, not just to JCL, instead wanting payment on delivery. The boating press had also been covering the 'revolutionary' boats being developed by JCL/Moonraker, with overall a good reception. However, Colin Chapman's drive for perfection was well known, as was the fact that the company was having difficulties in achieving both this and their sales targets. Arguably, such revolutionary technology is not as well received in the marine industry as elsewhere, due to the rather hostile testing ground of the high seas and sometimes hostile reception from the industry marine traditionalists. Although admiring of the design, potential boat buyers would often not 'take the risk' to buy anything really radical in design as they might do with a motor car. There is also a body of opinion, although the Mystere, Mamba and Mirage were aimed at the Mediterranean market, that they were far too radical in design. They required the buyer to 'take a risk' with new and, it time terms, untested designs .

The development of these new ideas were not only far too costly, but they took too long. By the time they had arrived on the market place, not only had the market changed but so had the competition who were also fighting for survival.

Another theory compares the methods of those companies who survived this period and JCL/Moonraker. It is fair to say that many companies were able to have an advantage in following JCL, in terms of technology and marketing. Many of their local competitors also operated hire fleets or holiday lets which provided some income over the lean years allowing survival. The six day launches kept at Brundall Gardens were disbanded after the first year and it became obvious that the desired planning consents would not be obtained, and hiring was never intended to be a business proposition. However, where the competition differed was how they packaged and furthered their development. For example, the Powles and Princess kept all their models named the same, they just made the boat bigger and changed some interior and design features. This kept the brand loyalty and allowed the customer to move with ease from one model to another, up and through the range. A Moonraker customer, once ready for a bigger boat had the option of the Marauder or Mystere, these were radically different in design and all too often the customer would move to a competitor's range and probably stay with that brand. The Moonraker was appealing to a different market to the company's other models, to the North European market as opposed to the Mediterranean market. Of course by now, the Moonraker was also not selling well enough to keep the company afloat as it was too small, especially in beam, for the modern tastes. Yet in 1973 John Berry had stated in the JCL 'in house' magazine that they had sold over one hundred Moonrakers in 1973 alone and their nearest rival was only achieving one third of Moonraker sales figures. The second hand Moonraker market was also very buoyant at this time and continues to be so. Norfolk Yacht Agency was based next door to the Bell Marine site and used to sell the 'traded in' Moonrakers on behalf of Moonraker/JCL. Jim Cole, who ran the company until recently, found that the Moonraker was always a good seller, but was reluctant to take the non-Moonraker models as they were more difficult to sell, with limited appeal in the UK as they were designed to sell to the Mediterranean market. Today, he states that there is still a good demand for a Moonraker 36 built after Colin Chapman's take-over.

There was a rumour that Moonraker had produced a 41 foot boat. This was started by an innovative and somewhat desperate sales team at Brundall Gardens in order to get customers to visit the yard. It did get customers to visit and did result in one or two sales. The Moonraker was indeed 41 foot long - measured from the extremities of the bow rails and davits rather than the hull !

There are those who strongly believe that if JCL and Chapman had just increased the beam of the Moonraker, produced a 42 foot version, with a few different model variants, then the company would still be in production and successful today. The costs of developing an existing model would not have been as high as they were with the Marauder, Mystere, etc. Despite their high development costs, the non-Moonraker models do now look a little dated in terms external styling details, such as windows etc., not surprising when you consider the age of the design and the fact that they were to the height of fashion. However, when looking at the hull shape, they have more in common with the designs of today than with their contemporaries of 30 years ago. This really demonstrates how far in advance of their time the design team were. The Moonraker was more of a traditional design and so does not appear to date in comparison. The Moonraker also appears to keep an emotional bond with it's past and present owners and has a strong following, with a thriving 'Moonraker Owners Club' in the UK and also in Denmark. Both have excellent web sites, and the Danish one averaged 900 hits per month during 2003, demonstrating the continued level of interest. There is also an International Moonraker Register which in 2003 started to collate the whereabouts of all the Moonrakers (contact Terje Dehn, Solvgade 9, 1th, DK-1307, Copenhagen, Denmark).

Above: Literally on the rocks, but Moonraker post JCL Marine was heading for the same fate.

Chapter Thirteen

Moonraker post JCL

After liquidation, some half finished Moonraker hulls were bought by a Norfolk Company called Waveney Lakes, who sold the finished 'Aquarian Dawn' – a Moonraker 36 (see Power Game – Moonraker on the rocks). The Moonraker moulds were then acquired by DC Marine in approximately 1986, again based in Vic Bell's Brundall boatyard. They started building the Moonraker 'Super' 36.

One of these was shown at the 1988 Southampton Boat Show by its distributors Monitor Marine which was formed to do this and run by former JCL General Manager, Robin Poulton and Stuart White, employing Bob Cornish as the production manager. This version of the Moonraker had a much updated interior and was powered by 2 185hp Perkins Diesels. The radar masts were aluminium and the windows were darkened. In fact the photograph shown from the front of the brochure was taken by Stuart White's publicity company, off the Isle of Wight on the way to the boat show. Bob Cornish is at the helm.

Only six were initially built from this boat show outing and five of these went to a company in Norway who sold them on. However, DC Marine took one of the Norwegian ones back as Norway had just had a huge recession, having been hit by the oil crisis. It was originally called 'Demon' and the owner refused to pay the VAT on the £96,000 selling price, so a legal battle waged over ownership for some five years. All this time the boat was shrink wrapped in Brundall to keep it safe. The affair was settled on appeal in the High Court, with DC Marine keeping 'Demon' to offset costs. The boat was finally sold to a farmer, who rarely used it, but it was kept in pristine condition. It has since changed ownership and been re-named 'M.Y. Ally's Dream'.

Vic Bell again bought the Moonraker mould tools from DC Marine in 1990 and built the last Moonraker in 1991 as a demonstrator. In reality he built it for himself so he built it with curved bulkhead interior finishes. He changed the engines to 2:1 rather than the traditional direct drive and used Mercury's so they were a lot quieter and faster, he also lowered the flybridge. He had the boat built by Excel Craft based on the river Orwell and so called the boat Excel. It was (in Vic's words) *'too good to keep on the river at Brundall'* so he sold it.

Some Moonraker enthusiasts disagree that Excel (later renamed Power Game) was in fact the last Moonraker. This is based on the argument that Bell had made some changes to the design and therefore the boat is not a 'true' Moonraker. Although understanding their point, as the Moonraker had been continually developed and adapted to new technology since it was first produced, this point is very debatable. According to the 'Moonraker International' magazine, produced by the UK branch of the Moonraker owners club, they believe the last 'true' Moonraker to be the last one built by Monitor Marine (this was in fact 'Demon' or 'M.Y. Ally's Dream'). It is an interesting story, whatever your point of view about which was the last 'true' Moonraker.

Other models post JCL

Colin Hamilton of Tamris Marine International Ltd bought the mould tools for the Mystere/Mirage. This company also later folded without producing any models and the Mirage mould tools (which had been left at Hethel) rotted. Pat Moss was engaged to cut up the Mirage tools.

The Mamba tools were also sold to Colin Hamilton and , under contract, Ian Willgress who produced at least one boat under the 'Falcon' label. The Marauder plans along with the 'Streaker' open sports boat (adapted Mamba) mould tools were sold to Davian Motor Marine Ltd, which traded as 'Cleopatra Ltd'. One rumour that a Marauder was refurbished after the companies were liquidated comes out of the fact that a Marauder owned by Padma Marine Ltd., effectively a dealer who bought the completed Marauder number 106, had sustained some damage hitting an unknown object out at sea. The 'refurbishment' was in fact repair of this damage paid for by the insurance company.

Moonraker on the rocks ! Power Game

In 2001, Vic Bell's Excel, renamed 'Power Game' by it's then owner Alan Waller, featured on the front page of the Sun newspaper, amongst others, in what is probably the most infamous Moonraker accident of all.

Waller had wanted a final cruise of all his favourite haunts and, as his wife didn't go with him, he advertised for a companion for the planned voyage in one of the yachting magazines. Mike Cant saw the advert and was interested as the itinerary was a fortnight's cruise to Guernsey, Jersey, up to France and possibly Cherbourg on the return.

Coincidently, Mike Cant owned Aquarian Dawn which was one of the last Moonrakers to be built from the JCL stable via Waveney Lakes. It had been launched on Saturday 19th June 1982, having been built for a Jim Hendon, who unfortunately had died, so it was bought by Ken Brown before Mike and his wife Noreen. Mike was surprised to find that the layout of the two boats was virtually identical, apart from the engines that Bell had put into the newer boat. He was also impressed with the finish on Bell's boat, with all the curved edges and the neat, tailored storage in the galley.

For the voyage, the two men went to Portsmouth to collect the boat before going to the Isle of Wight to fuel up, they moored up in the marina over night and set off at 6am in the morning. The previous evening Alan had put the charts out and was very confident about the trip as he had undertaken this on several occasions.

They were making good time, doing about 18 knots when they passed Alderney at 10:00 hrs. They left Alderney to Port, as Alan apparently usually left it to Port, and went in the way the big cats did. When they were approaching Guernsey, Alan made to turn in. At this point he started to have problems with the starboard engine, so speed was reduced to about 12 knots.

It was a very high tide and suddenly the boat stopped totally dead – from 12 knots. Mike was standing at the top of the companionway, and luckily was able to grab on to the rail to stop himself being thrown down the steps with force. There was a huge crash of loose items being hurled forward but, Mike later recounted, all the crockery and glasses in the lockers designed by Vic Bell stayed totally intact! Luckily neither man was badly hurt, beyond shock and a few cuts and bruises.

The lighthouse that they should have left to starboard had been left to Port, so the small keel on this very high tide had wedged the boat tight into a rock crevice.

The two men got into a dinghy amid a smell of diesel, as the tank had split on impact having been just filled up. A RIB came out from shore to rescue them and they were soon in the harbourmaster's office, where a salvage team were already assembled. Within ten minutes of leaving the boat, one salvage team had taken the props off, which then signalled 'their' salvage when the tide went down. It was a 10 meter tide so, when they hit the rock, it was only just below the surface, wedging on the small keel. The newspaper pictures do apparently, make the incident look worse than it was. Mike believes they were 'computer altered' as the lighthouse looks much closer in those photos. There is apparently quite a difference between the press photos and the private ones.

In Spring 2003, Power Game was advertised for sale again for £79,950.

Above: A surviving mould—awaiting the day when it will be used again?

Chapter Fourteen

The End?

After Bell's last build in 1991, no more Moonrakers were built. However it is a testament to their design, build, and quality, that today they sell well on the second hand market, still fetching good prices. There is a very active Danish Moonraker Owners Club and a subsidiary in the UK. The other makes built by JCL Marine are occasionally seen on the second hand boat market and also sell well.

The full contribution made to the marine industry by the involvement of Colin Chapman and his design, engineering, sales and management teams is probably equal to the contribution made to the motor trade. Certainly, after Moonraker/JCL's lead the marine industry started to see design led boats in the UK, especially in terms of reduced weight. The VARI technique, production line layout and marketing stance certainly influenced future developments in the mass produced boat market.

Today, the moulds and tools for the Moonraker 36 are back where they originated – in a corner of Bell's Marina in Brundall. Maybe that is a fitting end……..at least for the time being……………

Apendix A

The Brochures

The story of Moonraker and JCL Marine is a story of Collin Chapman and of his boats, but it is also a story of innovation, never more true than in the marketing and sales techniques that his team brought to the British motor boating industry.

The brochures produced to sell the boats demonstrate both the quality and functionality of the vessels, and they also demonstrate the marketing philosophy and techniques. Looking at the brochures today, they are unremarkable because they set a standard that is followed today. At they time when they were first employed, together with the highly professional presentation of products at boat shows, they were ground breaking in their industry.

Moonraker Stand at Earls Court 1973

At £10,000
those unforgettable days are not
only for the special few

Some people think we build the Moonraker Softrider 36 to give the loveliest lines, finest finish, and most elegant appointments in any seagoing yacht at anywhere near the price. But they're only half right. Instrumentation is comprehensive. Access to the engines easy. The superbly engineered hull, built to Lloyds-approved specification, providing that smooth, sure, soft-riding ability to go to sea safely.

Moonraker contains as standard many items which some manufacturers don't offer as extras. We put in controlled central heating, underlaid carpets, insulated ceilings and sides, illuminated cocktail bar, radio, TV, twin luxury flush toilet and shower suites, labour saving galley, fridge. With luxuriously comfortable berths for six or more, you don't get in each others way.

MOONRAKER softrider 36

Moonraker Marine International Limited, Brundall, Norwich, Sales Enquiries Telephone: John Standen, Brundall 3651.

Above: The Softrider was presented as a high performance boat with a luxury interior at an amazing package price. No need for lengthy trials or long study of optional specifications, just value for money and ready to go.

Above: All you need to know, an exciting high fashion and high performance motor boat. The assumptive sale concludes with the terms of sales and no need for technical specification.

EXPRESS CRUISER

EXPRESS SEDAN

SPORTS YACHT

Moonraker 36 leading data
Fitted Hull-Length   36′ 1″ (10.91 m)
O.A.L. Pulpit to
Davits When Fitted   40′ 6″ (12.03 m)
Beam   11′ 6″ (3.50 m)
Draft   3′ 0″ (0.91 m)
Standard Fuel   190 Imp. Galls.
                                       (904.5 litres)
Fresh Water   100 Imp. Galls. (477.3
                                       litres)

Water Line to
Cockpit Roof   8′ 3″ (2.51 m)
Weight Displacement   5.8/6.5 tons (5892/
                                       6604 Kg)
Thames Tonnage   16.43 tons approximately.
Speeds   8-21 Kts according to
                                       engine/s
Accommodation   5-9 persons
Construction   All GFRP monocoque.

MOONRAKER CLASS

Softrider 36′	Twin Diesels	Cruise-Max.
Cruiser	115 shp	8-12 Knots
Sedan	115 shp	8-12 Knots
Express Cruiser	175 shp	16-21 Knots
Express Sedan	175 shp	16-21 Knots
Sports Fisherman	175 shp	16-21 Knots
Sports Yacht	175 shp	16-21 Knots

Above: The Bell approach, offering multiple choice, small sketches and brief specifications.

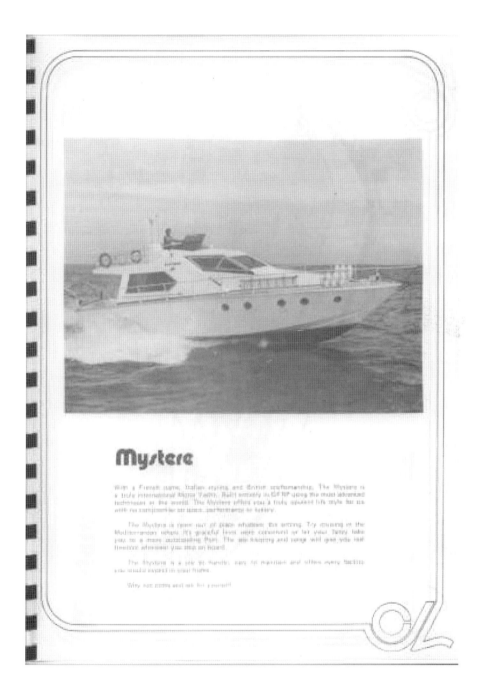

Mystere

With a French name, Italian styling and British craftsmanship, The Mystere is a truly international Motor Yacht. Built entirely in GRP using the most advanced techniques in the world. The Mystere offers you a truly upmarket life style for use with no compromise on space, performance or safety.

The Mystere is never out of place whatever the setting. Try cruising in the Mediterranean where it's graceful lines make convenient or let your family take you to a more outstanding Port. The sea keeping and range will give you the freedom wherever you stop on board.

The Mystere is a joy to handle, easy to maintain and offers every facility you could expect in your home.

Why not come and ask for yourself!

Above: The Mystere presented with an action shot and a sales description.

123

Above: The advertisement that summarizes the prime Moonraker market and the approach to presentation. Very wealthy and famous individuals purchased Moonrakers, but the core target market was successful professionals and businessmen, many coming to boating for the first time later in life.

NOW AVAILABLE FOR EARLY DELIVERY WORLDWIDE, THE OUTSTANDING MOONRAKER 36ft. 24kts. Convertable Accommodation for 6 Adults.
EXPORT AND AGENCY ENQUIRIES invited

MOONRAKER MARKETING, Brundall Gardens, Norwich, NR12 5RG, England
Tel: 0603 713856/714141 Telex: 97286

Above: A concise advertisement, combining the styles and logos in use, but with the emphasis on "Moonraker".

Below: Moonrakers were complete packages with a very comprehensive inventory of what were 'extras' for competitors.

Moonraker Super 36 Specification/Inventory

LOA 10.9m (36ft), Beam 3.5m (11ft 6ins), Draft 0.71m (2ft 4ins).
Fuel Capacity 909lt (200 galls), Water Capacity 410lt (90 galls), Dry Weight 7010kg (6.9 tons)

Hull and Deck
External exhaust system
Trim tabs
Sacrificial anodes
Dual tone horn
Stainless steel guard rail around boat
Bollards, 2 at stern, 2 at midships, 2 at bow
Position and navigation lights
6 pneumatic fenders with stowage hoops
Anodised aluminium escape hatch in forward deck
Stainless steel handrails on superstructure stop
Manual winch
Stainless steel stemhead fitting with anchor stowage
Anchor with 10 fathoms chain and 10 fathoms of warp
Davit mounting blocks
Socket for mains electric ship to shore line
Safety line wires
Antifouling
Stainless steel boarding ladder with GRP steps
Stainless steel fender baskets (4)

Flying Bridge
Secondary helm position pilots seat
Tachometers
Engine oil pressure gauges
2 water temperature gauges
Single lever throttle and gear controls
Seating for 5/6 with stowage beneath
Trim tab control, horn button
Spray deflector
Stainless steel handrails
Stainless steel ladder with GRP steps
Tonneau cover
Searchlight
Stainless steel radar mast

Engines
2 turbocharged Perkins 185 hp diesel engines
Manganese bronze 'P' brackets
17" x 15" 3-bladed propellors
Manganese bronze rudders
Transmission Borg Warner 1:1
Stainless steel 1½" shafts

Fore Cabin
Two beds with mattresses
Bedside lights
Escape hatch
Under bunk stowage
Carpet on hull sides
Teak bulkheads
Trimmed ceiling
Twin wardrobes

Forward Toilet
GRP shower tray with electric pump out
Curtain
Hot/cold shower mixer
Hot/cold taps in GRP basin
Sea toilet with pump out facility
Stowage under basin
Toothbrush holder
Towel rail
Toilet roll holder
Laminate on bulkheads and ceiling
Mirror
Electric shaving point
Electric lighting

Saloon
2 settees with bed under
Adjustable height table
Cocktail cabinet
Curtains
220V-24V-12V socket outlets
Under bunk stowage
Toughened tinted windows in black anodised aluminium frames
Teak bulkheads
Soft trim ceiling
Carpets on floors
Cabin lights over single beds
Forward divider

Wheelhouse
Folding pilots seat
4 person bench seat
Single lever throttle and gear controls
Tachometers
Sumlog
Ampmeters
Water temperature gauges
Engine oil pressure gauges
Gearbox oil pressure gauges
Trim tab control
Compass
Electrical control panel
Depth sounder
Auxiliary switch panel
Toughened tinted glass windows in black anodised aluminium frames
Engine starts and stops
2 Dudley wipers
Soft trimmed ceiling
Carpet
Curtains
Water contents gauge
Fuel contents gauge

Galley
Twin hob butane stove
2.8 cu ft 24V refrigerator
Sink unit with mixer taps
Two cupboards and drawer
Toughened tinted windows in black anodised aluminium frames
Curtains
Soft trimmed ceiling
Carpet
Overhead light
Wood veneered bulkheads
220V-24V socket outlets

Aft Stateroom
Double bed with mattress
Vanity unit
Toughened tinted glass windows in black anodised aluminium frames
Lights
Light over vanity unit
Under bunk stowage
Wardrobe
220V-24V socket outlets
Soft head lining
Carpet on floor
Mirror
Curtains
Teak bulkheads and soft trimmed bunk fronts
Drawer unit

Aft Toilet
GRP shower tray with electric pump out
Curtain
Hot/cold shower mixer
Hot/cold taps in GRP basin
Sea toilet with pump out facility
Stowage under basin
Towel rail
Toilet roll holder
Laminate on bulkheads and ceiling
Mirror
Electric shaving point
Electric lighting

Systems
Automatic fire extinguisher in engine bay with manual override
Hot water pressurised system with 10 gallon tank
Cold water pressurised system
Electric bilge pump in engine bay
Manual bilge pump in engine bay
Batteries with paralleling facility
Hydraulic steering at wheelhouse and flybridge positions

The manufacturers reserve the right to change specification/price without prior notification.

THE LAST CHORD

A while ago, you may recall, I featured an article entitled, 'The Lost Chord'. We had been searching for the first Moonraker ever built and wanted to know who now owned her and where she was. Well we got our answer, and we now know she is berthed in Dover.

Who though owns the last Moonraker ever built?

Well one could be forgiven for thinking that this distinction, falls to Alan Waller's 'Power Game'. True, 'Power Game' was the last one built but she is a bit of a hybrid, lower air draft and other modifications, all of which go to make her somewhat different to all that went before.

Well the last 'true to type' Moonraker has finally turned up, and what a story she could tell.

Her owner, Peter Marland has now joined the club and he wrote a line or two about the history of 'M.Y. Ally's Dream'.

'M.Y. Ally's Dream' moored in Boulogne

Originally named Demon, her first owner refused to pay the VAT on her, as he intended to moor her in Scandinavia. Demon was moved by road all over the country by Monitor Marine, to hide her from the owner who naturally wanted to take possession of her.

The legal battle lasted all of five years, and the boat became almost untouchable.

However a very expensive barrister finally resolved the issue and the boat was sold to a farmer in the Sussex region, who then moored her at Northerney for something like four years. During his stewardship she had only a couple of short runs, clocking up just 180 hours. Peter and Allison saw her at Northerney in pristine condition; fell in love with her, had a good survey done and they bought her.

Lack of use however had taken its toll on things like pumps and the odd bit of wiring but all these minor problems were soon put right, and on a visit to Boulogne over the Easter period, they had a great time, and were greatly impressed with the way 'M.Y Ally's Dream handled.

Above: There continues to be controversy about the 'last' Moonraker in the long line. Through the full life of the Moonraker, there were many updates and modifications. There were also several stages in the history of the ownership of production. For some, the only True Moonraker is one built during the Chapman years.

Appendix B

The Drawings

Moonraker and JCL Marine produced large quantities of drawings for design, planning, engineering and marketing. A number of these have been lost or have been stored away and forgotten.

This Appendix contains a selection of drawing that illustrate the range of activity and the models that made up the range.

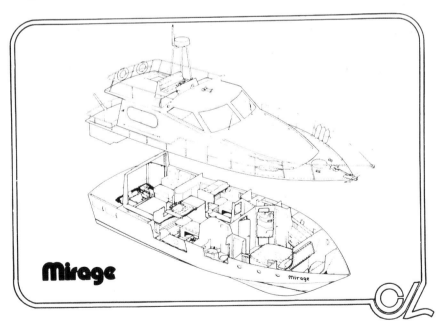

Above: A 3D drawing of the Mirage, showing the hull and super-structure mouldings and the internal arrangements.

EXPRESS CRUISER

EXPRESS SEDAN

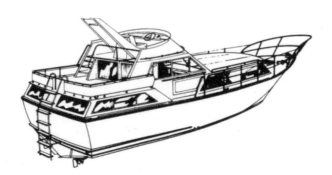

SPORTS YACHT

Above: The three Bell Boats classes

128

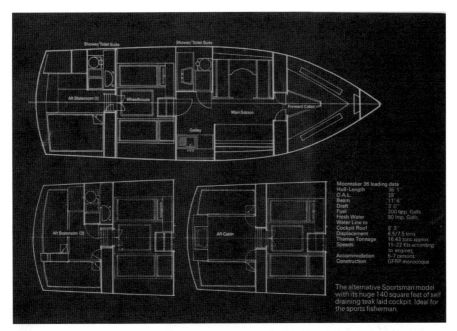

Above: Moonraker 36 alternative Sportsman model drawing.

Below: A 3D drawing of the Mystere from the boat manual.

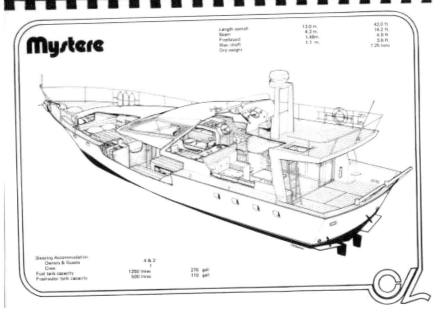

MAMBA

This is a high performance, top quality craft for the owner who seeks elegant styling with intimate accommodation. The saloon offers spacious facilities for daytime social activities and relaxation, augmented by a breakfast bar and well equipped galley. At night the saloon can be used to accommodate two extra guests on the large convertible bed settee if required. Below, the forward stateroom features a large double bed with private access to the toilet and shower. The whole interior decor has its emphasis on elegant furnishings, soft materials and diffused lighting of the very highest standards. All fixtures and fittings have been selected to harmonise with the interior and are among the finest available, worldwide.

THIS LEAFLET IS FOR BASIC INFORMATION ONLY. PLEASE ASK FOR FULL SPECIFICATION BOOKLET

Above: A 3D drawing of the Mamba.

Below Left: A floorpan drawing of the Mamba.

Below Right: A floorplan drawing of the Mamba Plus Two.

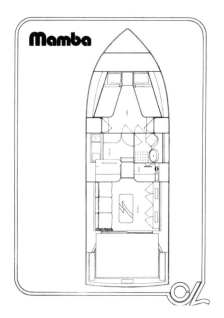

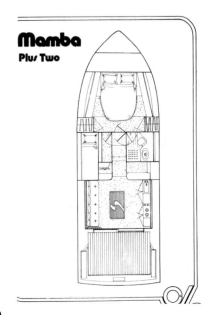

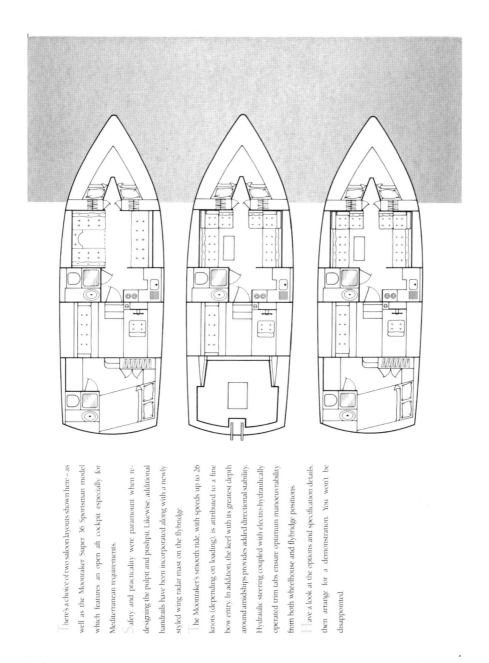

There's a choice of two saloon layouts shown here – as well as the Moonraker Super 36 Sportsman model which features an open aft cockpit especially for Mediterranean requirements.

Safety and practicality were paramount when re-designing the pulpit and pushpit. Likewise, additional handrails have been incorporated along with a newly styled wing radar mast on the flybridge.

The Moonraker's smooth ride, with speeds up to 26 knots (depending on loading), is attributed to a fine bow entry. In addition, the keel with its greatest depth around amidships provides added directional stability. Hydraulic steering coupled with electro-hydraulically operated trim tabs ensure optimum manoeuvrability from both wheelhouse and flybridge positions.

Have a look at the options and specification details, then arrange for a demonstration. You won't be disappointed.

Above: The Super 36 Sportsman was available in several package options. The drawings show three popular versions.

Above: A drawing described as Boat Plan 1

Centre: A very similar drawing described as Boat Plan 1 Small

Below: A surviving blueprint described as Boat Plan 4

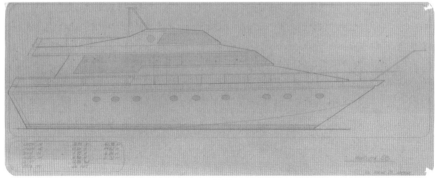

Glossary & Abbreviations

Aft – nautical term for back or rear of a vessel.

Beam – width of a boat at widest point.

Bilge – the lowest inner part of a ships hull, forming a transition between the bottom and the sides.

Buoy – a float moored in water to mark a location, warn of danger or indicate a navigational channel.

Chine – the line of intersection between the side and bottom of a flat bottom or v-bottom boat.

Constant velocity joint – a universal joint that allows power to be transmitted even at sharp angles.

Coracle – small rounded boat made of waterproof material stretched over wicker or wooden frames.

Davits – small crane or pulley over the side or end of a boat used to lift (and store) boats, anchors or cargo

Flybridge/Flying Bridge – the highest navigational bridge on a ship (often open) deck above the wheel house.

Helm – steering gear of a ship eg wheel or tiller.

Hull – the frame or body of a ship exclusive of mast, engines or superstructure.

Jig – device for holding machine work or a toll in place.

Keel – the principal structural member of a ship, running lengthways along the centre line from bow to stern. In traditional construction frames are attached to the keel. The keel often protrudes below the hull.

Le Mans – Annual (since 1906) 24 hour car race held in the north west French town of same name.

LRBC – Lloyd's Register Building Certificate.

Osmosis – diffusion of fluid through semi-permeable membrane.

Propshaft – the drive shaft, propeller shaft – often under the hull in marine vessels.

Roll and pitch – description of boats' motion in waves.

Skeg – the connection between the keel and stern post of a boat; an arm extending to the rear of the keel to support the rudder and protect the propeller.

Sloop – a single masted, fore and aft rigged sailing boat with a short standing bowsprit (or none) and a single headsail set from the forestay.

Superstructure – the parts of a ships structure above the main deck.

Transom – the aftermost structural member in a ship forming part of the stern.

Universal coupling – used for joining 2 shafts or parts of a machine endwise so one may give rotary motion to the other when forming an angle with it, or may move freely in all directions with respect to the other, as by means of a cross connecting the forked ends. Since this joint cannot act when the angle of the shafts is less than 140 degrees, a double joint of the same nature is used for lesser angles.

VARI – Vacuum assisted resin injection.

Wet Ride – the amount of spray or water coming onto the deck or onto the deck – as opposed to a 'dry ride'.

Bibliography

Although very little has been written about Colin Chapman's boats in published books, the local newspapers reported on Colin Chapman, his cars and his boats, because he was not only a significant figure, but his companies were significant employers in Norfolk. The archives of the local newspapers, now members of the Archant Group, provided valuable information and corroboration of other sources:

Eastern Daily Press and Eastern Evening News

Archant Group archives

Colin Chapman's design team were influenced by fast naval craft design and these influences are found in:

"Fast Fighting Boats 1870-1945. Their Design, Construction and Use" - Fock.

Although Colin Chapman's boats may have received little coverage in books, his life and his cars have received much attention:

"Lotus - A Formula One Team History" - Bruce Grant-Braham

"Colin Chapman: The Man and His Cars - The Authorised Biography" - Gerard Crombac

"Colin Chapman: The Wayward Genius" - Mike Lawrence

"Colin Chapman: Lotus Engineering - Theories, Designs and Applications" - Hugh Haskell

"The Piranha Club - power and influence in Formula One" - Timothy Collins

Index

H

Hamburg Boat Show – 85
Hamilton, Colin - 115
Hethel – 20, 42, 50, 58-60, 68, 69, 77, 85, 87, 97, 98, 101, 103, 109, 115
Huskisson, Robert – 61

I

Inchcape - 108
Industrial Marine Plastics Ltd – 24, 28, 37
International Moonraker Register - 111
Interplan Yachting - 91

J

Jacobs, John Colin Leslie – 47, 48
James and Caddy Ltd – 62
Jones, Ian - 59
JCL Marine Ltd – 19, 47-50, 62, 73, 94, 102, 107, 108, 113, 117, 119, 127

K

Kelly, John – 2
King, Warren – 43, 44, 45, 102

L

Lancer Marine Ltd - 44
Lane, David – 43, 63, 66, 78
Lloyds – 57, 61, 82
LRBC – 57, 58, 61, 81, 84
Ludham Plastics (Engineering) Ltd - 50

M

Maggini, Antonio – 83, 89
Mangusta – 13, 94, 107

Mamba – 80-83, 90-97, 107, 110, 115, 130
Marauder – 7, 50, 55, 59, 60, 64, 65, 69, 71-82, 86, 91, 96, 103, 107, 108, 110, 111, 115
Marauder Ltd – 50, 108
Martini – 92
Middleton, Ron – 63, 102
Microlights - 106
Mirage – 8, 83, 85, 89-99, 110, 115, 127
Mistral – 8, 92, 93, 107
Mogford, Leslie – 66, 79, 81, 85, 87, 88
Monitor Advertising - 33
Monitor Marine – 113, 114
Moonraker – 11, 17, 20-38, 40, 42-58, 60-65, 71, 72, 74, 77, 79, 81, 82, 95-99, 110-119, 129
Moonraker Marine Ltd – 23, 24
Moonraker Marine International Ltd – 61, 108
Moonraker Motor Yachts Ltd – 50, 108
Moss, Pat - 115
Mystere – 8, 50, 65, 69, 79, 80, 82-89, 94, 97, 107, 110, 111, 115, 129

N

Norfolk Yacht Agency - 111

P

Pardon, Paul – 85, 88
Pegasus – 47, 48, 49, 50
Percival, Tom – 92
Pestrell, Roger - 106
Putnam, Roger – 87, 88, 97
Poulton, Robin – 44, 113
Phillips, Roy – 79, 83, 92
Porter and Haylett - 71
Power Game – 114-116